The Burial-Places of Memory

The Burial-Places of Memory

Epic Underworlds in Vergil,

Dante, and Milton

RONALD R. MACDONALD

The University of Massachusetts Press

Amherst, 1987

Copyright © 1987 by The University of Massachusetts Press
All rights reserved
Printed in the United States of America
Set in Linotron Garamond No. 3 at Rainsford Type
Printed by Cushing-Malloy and bound by John Dekker & Sons

Library of Congress Cataloging-in-Publication Data

Macdonald, Ronald R., 1943–
The burial-places of memory.

Bibliography: p.
Includes index.
1. Epic poetry, European—History and criticism.
2. Hell in literature.   3. Voyages to the otherworld in
literature.   4. Virgil. Aeneis.   5. Dante Alighieri,
1265–1321. Divina commedia.   6. Milton, John, 1608–1674.
Paradise lost.   I. Title.
PN1333.H45M3   1987   809.1'3   86-19216
ISBN 0-87023-558-3

FOR MARIAN

dux femina facti

Contents

Acknowledgments

"There ain't nothing more to write about," Huck Finn says in concluding the narrative of his adventures, "and I am rotten glad of it, because if I'd a knowed what a trouble it was to make a book I wouldn't a tackled it and ain't agoing to no more." Like Huck, I too am "rotten glad" that this book is finished, but unlike him I am far less sure that "there ain't nothing more to write about," and so I offer no promises about not trying it again. Definitive closure in a project like the one that follows is necessarily an impossibility; finished it may be (in whatever arbitrary sense), completed it will never be. What follows is offered as a series of suggestions, some of which at least I hope the reader will find provocative, hints, though I am sorry to say in Wordsworth's phrase, no "monumental hints." Anyone who undertakes a project of this sort is in the position not so much of Huck Finn but of Cervantes' Gines de Pasamonte, who when asked by Don Quixote if his book, *The Life of Gines de Pasamonte*, is finished, replies with unassailable logic, "How can it be finished if my life isn't?"

That trouble of making a book which leaves one so rotten glad when it is done nevertheless brings with it some happy associations and the generous advice and assistance of friends and colleagues, a few of whom it is my pleasure to acknowledge here.

Thalia Pandiri, William Oram, and Robert Petersson have all been a constant source of encouragement, while dispensing generously their ideas about Vergil and Milton. Charles Henderson, whose knowledge of Latin is unsurpassed in my experience, and George Dimock, whose command of the Homeric poems is impressive to the point of being uncanny, offered me advice of technical depth and on not a few occasions—with grace and the greatest good will—simply set me straight. I have benefited in ways that perhaps they cannot imagine from the conversation of Jackson Wilson, an imaginative literary critic and philosopher (he has also been known to write history), and Paul Pickrel, whose ideas about and essays upon nineteenth-century English fiction have proved surprisingly pertinent to my attempt to talk about epic. Leslie Brisman paid a great deal of thoughtful attention to an early version of the manuscript and gave me eminently sound advice. Steven Mullaney did the same. Arthur Kinney not only paid careful attention but became a virtual sponsor: my debt to him is great and still growing. Camille Paglia, who read portions of the manuscript at various stages, has been not only a valuable source of advice but also a true friend.

Grateful acknowledgment is made to Random House for permission to quote *The Aeneid of Virgil*, translated by Robert Fitzgerald, copyright © 1981, 1982, 1983 by Robert Fitzgerald; to Harper and Row for permission to quote selections from *The Odyssey of Homer*, translated by Richmond Lattimore, copyright © 1965, 1967 by Richmond Lattimore; and to The University of Chicago Press to quote *The Iliad of Homer*, translated by Richmond Lattimore, copyright © 1951 by The University of Chicago Press.

The person to whom this book is dedicated presided over its emergence, encouraged its progress, and suffered with patience the pressure of its completion. I have asked her many times, *Musa, mihi causas memora*, and she has never failed me: *vera incessu patuit dea*.

The Burial-Places of Memory

Introduction

THERE is a remarkable and triumphant moment late in the fourth act of *Antony and Cleopatra* when Antony, convinced that Cleopatra has killed herself, and inspired by what he takes to be her courage, determines forthwith to join her in the otherworld:

> I will o'ertake thee, Cleopatra, and
> Weep for my pardon. So it must be, for now
> All length is torture; since the torch is out,
> Lie down and stray no farther. Now all labor
> Mars what it does; yea, very force entangles
> Itself with strength. Seal then, and all is done.
> Eros!—I come, my queen!—Eros!—Stay for me!
> Where souls do couch on flowers, we'll hand in hand,
> And with our sprightly port make the ghosts gaze.
> Dido and her Aeneas shall want troops,
> And all the haunt be ours. Come, Eros, Eros!
>
> (4.14.44–54)[1]

It makes surprisingly little difference in the long run that Antony's vision is elicited by a report that isn't true: what we respond to is the intensity of his imagination, his address to the absent queen, quite as if she could hear him and respond to him as literally as the servant whom he summons from offstage.

The spectacle of the living warrior moving through a crowd of pale and bloodless shades, resplendent in his armor, is a familiar one in the epic tradition, from Homer's Odysseus in the eleventh *Odyssey* with his gleaming sword; through Vergil's Aeneas in the sixth *Aeneid*, as the shades scatter before the luminous hero and raise a thin, barely audible cry; to Dante's pilgrim in the *Commedia*, who leaves footprints and casts shadows in the land of the weightless and transparent dead. Perhaps we witness the tradition of the motif in the process of extinction, and a fully self-conscious farewell to it, as Milton's Satan, who shines with some of his original glory at the beginning of *Paradise Lost*, slowly fades into the visible darkness of Hell. Shakespeare contrives the vivid presence of his protagonists among the dead by exploiting the Anglo-Saxon layer of English on the one hand and the Romance layer on the other. He might have written, preserving both meaning and scansion, "And with our ghostly port make the sprites gaze," but only at the price of reversing figure and ground and destroying the effect of the brilliant Antony and Cleopatra walking hand in hand among the throng of plebeian shades.

The strict neoclassicist will detect a blunder in these lines, comparable to the striking of the clock in *Julius Caesar* or the mention of Aristotle at the siege of Troy in *Troilus and Cressida*. The *Aeneid* does not, as a matter of fact, tell us that Dido and Aeneas are united in death, as Antony's great vision implies. Shakespeare seems to have forgotten about Sychaeus. But the strict neoclassicist would do well to push forward in all consistency. Antony delivers his speech on the field of the Battle of Actium in 31 B.C. He cannot very well be alluding to a poem that never saw the light until after the author's death in 19 B.C., a poem that was in any case scarcely more than an idea forming in Vergil's mind in 31.

But there is much more than inadvertence or a cavalierly antihistorical attitude at work in Shakespeare's lines; they are in fact a signal example of some of the ways the poet manages the burden of the tradition in which he finds himself working. We willingly revise our first assumption—that Shakespeare is alluding to the *Aeneid* through the person of Antony—and grant that Antony in 31 B.C. is imagining, creating in his own right. By setting his scene in a time when the *Aeneid* was not yet written, Shakespeare reminds us of the historical status of the Roman poem, of the time when its authority could not loom large, because it could not loom at all. He puts us in mind not only of its origin, but of the fact that it *had* an origin and was not simply handed down mysteriously from on high. History for Shakespeare is not a unified story transmitted by a few privileged texts about which there is simple consensus. He reveals it rather as a diverse collection of points of view, sometimes a chaos of contradictory interpretations in competition, all enacting their several claims to authority. The time when the *Aeneid* was not yet written was also the time when what would prove its meliorist view of the events leading up to what we would come to call the *pax romana* (under the man who was rechristened "Augustus" after the fact) must have seemed doubtful indeed. History is not a closed record, for those events are *still* available for interpretation, and in revealing the *Aeneid* not as history, but in its undeniable historicity, Shakespeare claims the sovereign right of the poet to create his own version of events, a right that does not descend to him *from* Vergil, for he shares that right *with* Vergil from the beginning. The poet's imagination is no more bound by Vergil's version of history than Antony's imagination of Dido and Aeneas is bound by a poem that does not yet exist. Why not a version in which Antony and Cleopatra emerge as hero and heroine? Why should that version be any more or less authoritative than Vergil's tale of the triumphant Augustus? If all depends on what we mean by "triumphant," why not stand the *Aeneid* on its head?

Shakespeare uses the otherworld here to effect a remarkable dispersion of authority. Vergil's massive presence in the tradition, a presence amounting to a hegemony, is viewed in such a way as to make it seem once again relative, a point of view among other competing points of view. Shakespeare's stance is not, strictly speaking, revisionist, if we mean that in depriving Vergil of absolute authority he then awards it to himself. He only asks us to see history as open, a collection of meanings in competition, in which there is still room for other voices, for the insertion of fresh perspectives and emphases. Shakespeare knew that language, the medium of history, is a "preconstrained" phenomenon: it comes to us already laden with assumptions and interpretations which it is the poet's job to reveal *as* assumptions and interpretations. In thus interrogating his language the poet is like Cleopatra interrogating the messenger about Antony's marriage to Octavia (2.5). She refuses to accept his simple—and apparently incontrovertible—assertion, "He is married," as anything but the language of prose, those words whose meanings are guaranteed by a tacit agreement of the social order. She knows with Shakespeare of a marriage of true minds to which she will not admit impediments, and, if she never does "marry" Antony in the sense the messenger intends, so that in one way her line at the end, "Husband, I come" (5.2.287), flies in the face of common sense, there are yet few who would deny that her courage proves her title to the name. Cleopatra knows that if all she does is to receive messages from Rome, she ceases to be a queen. We might add that if all the poet does is to use words just in the (common) senses that society and tradition supply, he ceases to be a poet.

Though Shakespeare is in every way extraordinary, he is not

anomalous. The poets treated in the present essays similarly interrogate their language, their traditions, and their predecessors
in the epic genre. Vergil, Dante, and Milton are all engaged in
effecting historical reversals, in questioning the order that chronological and narrative history dictates, and they begin with the
Land of the Dead. Of Milton's poetry Macaulay memorably remarked that "it acts like an incantation":

> Its merit lies less in its obvious meaning than in its occult power.
> There would seem, at first sight, to be no more in his words than
> in other words. But they are words of enchantment. No sooner
> are they pronounced, than the past is present and the distant near.
> New forms of beauty start at once into existence, and all the burial-
> places of memory give up their dead.[2]

The language the poet receives is indeed a "burial-place," a collective memory laden with assumptions and ideologies. These he
must bring to consciousness, if he is to turn the received language
into an instrument peculiarly his own. Shelley thought that all
language near the source contained the chaos of a cyclic poem.
The epic poet, working in a narrow tradition with only a very
few indisputably great exemplars, worries more specifically not
about the ancient corpse of an anonymous cyclic poem lying on
the bottom of language (*it* can be expected to remain submerged
until the final trumpet), but about his predecessors in epic, all
too un-anonymous, whose works still stamp the language with
their unmistakable impress.

In asserting that the poet begins with the land of the dead, I
am concerned neither with where the episode occurs in the order
of the finished poem, nor with first lines and invocations, the
beginnings of texts as we encounter them on the page. I am
concerned with the more speculative question of the process of
creation, with the primal meditation that makes textual beginnings possible in the first place. There is a kind of logic, amount-

ing almost to a necessity, in meditating first on the Land of the Dead, which reduces the hierarchy of priority yielded by the serial narrative of history to simultaneousness. In the underworld all pasts are made equally present. This reduction provides an opportunity for a fresh start, in effect, a chance to discover a new order in the past, in which the voice of the present has an authentic claim to be heard. Once all pasts are equally present, the poet may then represent the past as *genuinely* past, as over and done with. "One has patience with every kind of living thing," Emerson wrote in his journal, "but not with the dead alive."[3] All three poets treated here, I would like to speculate, asked themselves a version of Emerson's question about a "retrospective" age that confines itself to building "the sepulchres of the fathers":

> The foregoing generations beheld God and nature face to face; we, through their eyes. Why should not we also enjoy an original relation to the universe? Why should not we have a poetry and philosophy of insight and not of tradition, and a religion by revelation to us, and not the history of theirs? Embosomed for a season in nature . . . why should we grope among the dry bones of the past, or put the living generation into masquerade out of its faded wardrobe?[4]

The land of the dead is thus an arena where the poet can contemplate the past *as* past, where, to use Freud's terminology, he can *remember* the past without being obliged to repeat it.[5] The underworld is in this respect analogous to the unconscious, and the journey there has something like the effect of liberating the poet from repressed material that he would otherwise have to repeat. "The ditty does remember my drown'd father," says Ferdinand of Ariel's haunting song in *The Tempest*:

> Full fadom five thy father lies,
>   Of his bones are coral made:

> Those are pearls that were his eyes:
>> Nothing of him that doth fade,
> But doth suffer a sea-change
> Into something rich and strange.
> Sea-nymphs hourly ring his knell.
>> (1.2.397–403)

I take "remember" here literally, in the sense of re-member, give new members, replace eyes with pearls and bones with coral. Some such act of re-membrance is what the epic poet aims at, to hear the nymphs ring the predecessor's knell, even as they turn him into something rich and strange. Rich *and* strange: what is required—and it is in many ways a paradoxical requirement—is that the predecessor yield up his riches at the same time that he keep his distance. We might recast Macaulay's remark about Milton's poetry to include Dante and Vergil as well: not only is the past present and the distant near, but the present must become past and the near (the all-too-near) distant.

For true remembering, as opposed to compulsive repetition, is the only way the past can be experienced as masterable. Simonides of Ceos, we are told in the *De oratore* of Cicero (2.86), invented the technique that would come to be known as the art of memory. Simonides, who had been providentially summoned from a banqueting hall the roof of which had collapsed in his absence, was able to identify the victims, mangled beyond recognition, by their places at the table. The legend founded what proved to be a long-lived tradition of memorizing speeches by associating their elements, or images standing for their elements, with the physical locations within edifices, actual or imagined. The rhetor would then revisit the locations in imagination, following a predetermined ambit, and require the locations to yield up in order their memorial contents.[6] Epic underworlds may be related to this venerable mnemonic technique, they may in fact contain the reminiscence of a technique of reminiscing. And yet the "places" of memory (the technical term for both Cicero and the anonymous author of the rhetorical treatise called *Ad Herrenium* is *loci*) become the burial-places of memory only with the supervention of the idea of repression, an *active* forgetting, so to speak, as opposed to the merely passive decay of the memory trace. It is the psychoanalytic *ars memoriae* that the following chapters primarily address.

These chapters treat three different, but intimately related, aspects of the poet's act of re-membrance. Remembering Homer is for Vergil largely a matter of "foregrounding"[7] his own poem against the Homeric world, which is rendered as a pale backdrop, rather in the way the resplendent Aeneas appears among the thin shades of the fallen Greeks in the sixth book:

> at Danaum proceres Agamemnoniaeque phalanges
> ut videre virum fulgentiaque arma per umbras,
> ingenti trepidare metu; pars vertere terga,
> ceu quondam petiere rates, pars tollere vocem
> exiguam: inceptus clamor frustratur hiantis.
>
> (6.489–93)

> Not so
> Agamemnon's phalanx, chiefs of the Danaans:
> Seeing the living man in bronze that glowed
> Through the dark air, they shrank in fear. Some turned
> And ran, as once, when routed, to the ships,
> While others raised a battle shout, or tried to,
> Mouths agape, mocked by the whispering cry.
>
> (657–63)[8]

It is probably no accident that Vergil conceives of the shades of Homeric warriors here as barely able to speak: their scanty cry mocks their gaping mouths, and those who were formerly described as "of the great war cry" have now only a *vox exigua*.

It is arguable, and, indeed, has been argued, that preliterate man can have no real sense of a past.[9] The oral bard may believe that he is singing not only the same poem he has sung before, but also the same poem his ancestors sung before him, though we know that this can scarcely be the case. He has, after all, no written record of the past to compare with his own performance. The world for him has always been in its important respects much the same, and he has every reason to believe that it will remain so. Lacking as he does a real sense of a past, preliterate man must also lack a real sense of a future. But the intervention of writing changes things utterly. The presence of records provides important evidence of differences between then and now, and literate man not only knows for the first time the past as past, he conceives of a time when his own situation will be past, which is to say that he conceives of a future. It is certainly not the case that preliterate cultures lack history: any culture is, willy-nilly, historical. But it seems likely that they do lack the *concept* of history, for in the absence of a written record it is difficult to imagine how they would acquire it. Writing is more than an enabling technology, for beyond its unquestionable usefulness, it is evidently something to think with. Among other things, it enables man to think of history. The fact that Vergil *wrote* the *Aeneid* is very likely one of the most important things we know about it.

I speculate that at bottom Vergil's techniques for dealing with Homer rested on his consciousness of his own historical consciousness. Whatever one may say about Homer's plenitude of vision, his celebrated concreteness, and his particularity in the here and now, his vision *remains* in the here and now, yielding a world of eternal return in an unending cycle of fullness and loss. The scenes on the shield of Achilles, described in the magnificent ecphrasis of the eighteenth *Iliad*, scenes of daily toil, battle, marriage rites, and sacrifice, betray no consciousness of historical process, of previous evolution leading toward this moment, or of subsequent evolution leading away from it. The idea of an *eschaton* was foreign to Homer, and it is precisely the idea of the *eschaton*, that the present exists *for* a time in the future, that enabled Vergil to begin extricating himself from the Homeric past. One has only to compare Vergil's own ecphrasis (8.626–728) describing the shield of Aeneas with its *res Italae* and *Romanorum triumphi* to see how much his thoroughly historical thought distinguishes him from Homer. There is thus a certain rationale (it would be imprudent to call it justice) in the fact that the shades of the Homeric warriors in the *Aeneid* are excluded from the process which is Rome and do not participate in the recirculation of souls that Anchises describes later in the book. Indeed, the Greeks among the Homeric shades are those who have attempted to extirpate the Trojan seed. They are the arch-enemies of Roman eschatology.

If Vergil works with the past primarily by foregrounding the present and future, Dante works with it by making the bold gesture of including it whole.[10] The dead return in the *Commedia* not as intruders, but at the express invitation of the poet. A subdivision of Dante's lowest circle of Hell is reserved for those who have been treacherous to guests (*Inf.* 33.91–157), and one way of understanding Dante's extraordinary gesture of including the past so openly in his poem might be to say that, like his own Fra Alberigo (109–50), he invites his poetic kindred to dinner in order to slay them. We will see that there is some truth in this formulation, though we will not overlook the astonishing degree to which the Vergil of the *Commedia* is the historical Vergil and not the phantom of medieval science fiction. Meanwhile, it is important to stress the impression of impartial fairness the *Commedia* conveys: the poem is open to ancients and moderns alike, and they are often made to consort in arresting combinations. In *Inferno* 30, for instance, Griffolino of Arezzo and Gianni Schicchi of Florence (two notorious confidence men contemporary

with Dante), Master Adamo of Brescia (the most skillful counterfeiter of the florin in Dante's day), Potiphar's wife (Gen. 39:6–
20), and Sinon (*Aeneid* 2) are all found together in the last ditch
of the eighth circle. This altogether heterogeneous collection
makes a basic and (for Dante) surprisingly ahistorical point: fraud
and falsification are fraud and falsification whether committed by
ancient or modern. Evil ignores temporal sequence, and to have
come first is of no avail in Hell. Dante pursues a technique that
amounts to a revision of historical understanding, for from the
otherworldly perspective history generates not an aristocracy
based on old blood, but a meritocracy based on probity.

To say that Dante puts the past in dialogue with the present
in the *Commedia* is more than to use a figure of speech: he places
ancients and moderns in literal dialogue and has them compete
on even ground. But to deny that the context is not ultimately
weighted in favor of the modern would be to assert more than
the facts of the poem will warrant. Dante's invitation to the dead
is, finally, an ambivalent one, for it is aimed at mastering the
masters. There is a surprising moment in *Paradiso* 20, when Dante
is viewing the souls comprised by the eye of the imperial eagle.
Those in the eye are the highest rank of the just rulers, and
we are not startled to find David, Hezekiah, Trajan, Constan-
tine, and William the Good among them. It is puzzling, however,
to find the pagan Ripheus. There can be no doubt that Dante
had his eye on Vergil here, because Ripheus is known only
through the *Aeneid* and is mentioned there in only one brief
passage:

> 'cadit et Ripheus, iustissimus unus
> qui fuit in Teucris et servantissimus aequi
> (dis aliter visum).'   (2.426–28)

> "and Ripheus fell,
> A man uniquely just among the Trojans,

The soul of equity; but the gods would have it
Differently."   (560–63)

Dante's extraordinary revision of the Vergilian vision is plain
enough. Ripheus may have "seemed otherwise" (the literal sense
of Vergil's phrase *dis aliter visum*) than the most just to Vergil's
gods, but in the sight of the God who is the light of the world
he has his reward. The sense of a gloomy and inscrutable fatality
implicit in Vergil's phrase is dispelled at a stroke. "Now he knows
much of the divine grace that the world cannot see" (70–71),[11]
says the eagle of Ripheus. He knows more, and, we might add,
Dante knows more, than the poet who first recorded his name.

The final chapter suggests, following the lead of Harold Bloom,
that Milton found his primary defense against the past in the
trope of metalepsis and that *Paradise Lost* is in a special sense a
meditation on priority.[12] Bloom expands the traditional rhetorical
definition of metalepsis (for Quintilian it is simply the meto-
nymical substitution of one word for another which is itself figurative) to mean the poet's substitution of himself and his poem
for his predecessors in the place of priority. Bloom's sense of the
trope preserves one of the meanings of the Greek *lambanein*, "to
make one's own." Greek *metalepsis* means "a partaking of, a com-
munion in a thing." Coming as he did, and for whatever reasons,
at the end of the epic tradition, Milton needed a way of claiming
precedence, of making the past speak for him and of him, and,
in insisting that his story, if not his poem, is the first (and in
some sense the only) story ever told, Milton manages to convey
something like the impression that previous epics were really
trying to tell the story of *Paradise Lost* with very partial success.
It is only apparently a paradox that in choosing the story furthest
back in the past, the story of origins, Milton claims the future
and achieves a conspectus of all history from Creation to Last
Judgment.

Paradise Lost is a poem both haunted and haunting, on the one hand a vast echo chamber where phrases fall with uncanny familiarity on the ear, on the other a strikingly original poem (in two senses: it returns to origins, and it seems altogether unprecedented) where those phrases return with alienated majesty to persuade us that their purport was always something different from what their first authors intended:

> Not that fair field
> Of *Enna*, where *Proserpin* gath'ring flow'rs
> Herself a fairer Flow'r by gloomy *Dis*
> Was gather'd, which cost *Ceres* all that pain
> To seek her through the world; nor that sweet Grove
> Of *Daphne* by *Orontes*, and th' inspir'd
> *Castalian* Spring might with this Paradise
> Of *Eden* strive; nor that *Nyseian* Isle
> Girt with the River *Triton*, where old *Cham*,
> Whom Gentiles *Ammon* call and *Lybian Jove*,
> Hid *Amalthea* and her Florid Son,
> Young *Bacchus*, from his Stepdame *Rhea's* eye;
> Nor where *Abassin* Kings thir issue Guard,
> Mount *Amara*.   (4.268–81)[13]

The very plenitude of citation here, the superabundance of example, makes Milton's point: all poets try to speak of Paradise, but in the multiplicity of fallen tradition, in the Babel-babble that human language has become, they lose sight of the unitary, real, compelling garden at the center of Milton's poem that was—and can never be again.

My categories are proximate and are not meant to be mutually exclusive. Clearly foregrounding requires inclusion, as inclusion will inevitably involve foregrounding. The trope of metalepsis requires them both. Vergil, Dante, and Milton are treated here in chronological order. By so arranging them I intend no judgment of value, no theory of steady progress over the centuries toward ever more efficient ways of controlling the past. It is perhaps a hallmark of genuine historical thinking that it denies such neat progressions and comforting symmetries, and, in any case, I understand the problems here discussed as perennial rather than as finally soluble. They have to be assumed afresh in each return to the epic tradition. Neither Vergil nor Dante nor Milton can provide unequivocal answers; they can, however, offer a rich variety of perspectives on the problems.

I

Vergil: The Easy Descent

From Avernus

SINCE the work of Milman Parry radically changed our understanding of the composition and reception of the Homeric corpus, so much has been said and written about the differences between oral and written literature that it may seem superfluous—or worse—to add anything more. But by way of introducing this study of Vergil's *Aeneid* and its sixth book, let me meditate briefly not on the relatively arcane matters of formula as opposed to free invention, of mnemonic technique as opposed to writerly craft, but on the central and obvious matter of telling stories. It seems inevitable that both Homer and Vergil thought of themselves (among other things) as storytellers and that each possessed attitudes, richly implied in the poetry, toward the role of storyteller and the institution of storytelling.

That the act of narration is not only a procedure in the *Aeneid* and in the *Odyssey* (which I choose to discuss here because storytelling is so much more central to this poem than it is to the *Iliad*), but is also in both cases an important theme, is revealed in the fact that both poems contain conspicuous examples of embedded narration, stories within the stories that are in all instances more than a formal device for bringing the reader or listener up to date or otherwise giving him the broader picture. The hero of the *Odyssey* is, to be sure, a brilliant teller of tales in his own right, able to improvise an authoritative story of personal origins (whether true or false) with all the skill we attribute to the bard who is in the act of telling us about Odysseus telling a story. And the hero of the *Aeneid*, though scarcely as voluble, nor, we may be tempted to say, as skillful as his Homeric predecessor, is nonetheless involved on one central occasion occupying Vergil's second and third books in telling the story of his origins and explaining his presence in a rising African kingdom. The narrative act is very evidently thematized in both poems through the technique of embedded narration, set apart and interrogated. And in each case the interrogation may reveal some instructive differences.

LET US TURN for the moment to Odysseus, and not initially to his virtuoso account of his wanderings in Books 9–12, but to the lesser (although strategically crucial) yarns he spins for Athena and the swineherd Eumaeus in the thirteenth and fourteenth books. The first is of course the cautiously mendacious account he gives the goddess, who is disguised as a young shepherd, of where he has come from and what he is up to. Odysseus pretends to be a Cretan in flight from Orsilochus, son of Idomeneus, whom, as he says quite truthfully, he has refused deference and service at Troy. Athena, who knows perfectly well with whom she is talking, seems delighted by the deviousness of her protégé:

So he spoke. The goddess, gray-eyed Athene, smiled
    on him,
and stroked him with her hand, and took on the shape
    of a woman
both beautiful and tall, and well versed in glorious
    handiworks,
and spoke aloud to him and addressed him in winged
    words, saying:
"It would be a sharp one, and a stealthy one, who
    would ever get past you
in any contriving, even if it were a god against you.
You wretch, so devious, never weary of tricks, then
    you would not
even in your own country give over your ways of
    deceiving
and your thievish tales. They are near to you in your
    very nature."   (13.287–95)[1]

Athena is quite right: *mythoi klopioi*, thievish and artful tales, *are*
at the bottom of the hero's heart. The passage, like so many
others in the *Odyssey*, is rather clearly a celebration not only of a
story well told, but of a story that will work in the circumstances.
And it can scarcely be inconsequential that Athena transforms
herself into a woman "beautiful and tall, and well versed in
glorious handiworks," for effective storytelling is a kind of
handiwork in itself, as important in these circumstances as, say,
skill with a bow. Here, as elsewhere, it is Homer's preeminently
instrumental sense of narration that is to the fore.

    Odysseus's next narration on returning to Ithaca is the long
and complicated hard-luck story he spins for Eumaeus in the
fourteenth book (191–359). This saga of wandering and storm
and hard fighting and bondage is undoubtedly inspired by Odysseus's own sufferings, that is, it is a lie that bears a certain relation

to truth and tends, even more than its predecessor, to raise the difficult problem implicit in much of the *Odyssey* of disentangling the one from the other. It is surely important in context that in one sense Eumaeus's response to the yarn is upside down or backward: he firmly disbelieves what is undoubtedly true in the narrative and appears to believe what is undoubtedly false. He has had experience with vagabonds who try to curry favor with Penelope and Telemachus by bearing false tales of Odysseus's return (121–47), and thus, though he accepts the Cretan son of Castor and his tale of woe, he firmly refuses any consoling news of Odysseus's imminent return.

One of the interesting effects of this pair of brilliantly contrived stories in the larger context of the poem is retrospective, for we are scarcely meant to forget as we embark on the second half of the poem that Odysseus has just come from a far more prominent and perhaps more consequential occasion of storytelling among the Phaeaecians. It would be unwise to propose that the mendacious stories in Books 13 and 14 call into question the veracity of the great narration that occupies virtually all of Books 9–12. Odysseus is the sole authority for what is said there, and even if we have reason to question it, we surely lack the means. But we may find a certain retrospective unsettling of the notion that the great performance in the halls of Alcinous is simply an extension of the entertainment already under way, although Odysseus himself does something to encourage this view, and for excellent reasons:

> "O great Alkinoos, pre-eminent among all people,
> surely indeed it is a good thing to listen to a singer
> such as this one before us, who is like the gods in his
>   singing;
> for I think there is no occasion accomplished that is more
>   pleasant
> than when festivity holds sway among all the populace,

and the feasters up and down the houses are sitting in order
and listening to the singer, and beside them the tables are
   loaded
with bread and meats, and from the mixing bowl the wine
   steward
draws the wine and carries it about and fills the cups. This
seems to my own mind to be the best of occasions." (9.2–11)

This expansive ceremonial gesture should not obscure for us the
fact that from Odysseus's point of view this is a rhetorical occasion,
that the larger purpose of his whole account, whether it is true or
false, is to get the Phaeaecians to intervene and, in effect, to complete the story he has perforce left unfinished. It is difficult to
imagine in these circumstances an Odysseus who simply abandons
himself to the memory of his wanderings, like a method actor becoming one with his role. This is a man with at least one eye on
the house, weaving a complex and highly self-conscious effect
with the set purpose of getting himself restored to Ithacan shores.

   It works, of course. As the story catches up with its own
present, the Phaeaecians are induced to complete it in experience
and convey Odysseus, laden with gifts, to his Ithacan home. *That*
is the last episode in the story known as the Wanderings of
Odysseus. Such smooth and perfect harmonization of narration
and experience, where the one completes the other; a world where
an experience can complete a story and stories are constantly being
elicited by experience; a world where a scar, for instance, a seam
in the otherwise smooth surface of things, immediately calls forth
a digressive story of how it came to be—this proliferation of
narrative giving onto experience and experience onto narrative
must make us wonder if for Homer the categories of doing something and telling about doing something were quite so distinct
and water-tight as they have come to seem to us. We may guess
that they were not, and that for good reason. For without con-

ceding too much to the view of the Homeric poems as ency-
clopedic repositories,[2] we can at least admit that Homer must
have been closely in touch with a way of thinking that understood
narratives as modes of intervention in daily affairs. When so much
of the vital work of a culture is accomplished through narrative—
the transmission of wisdom, technique, genealogy, procedure—
it must seem that to tell something *is* to do something, and
something important. Like the distinction between truth and
falsehood, the distinction between doing and telling may be a
difficult one to make. Perhaps the first question to put to a
Homeric story is not what it means, but what in the circumstances
it does. We may readily suspect that this is the first question the
man of many ways asks of a story, for if the Phaeaecians, whose
way of life is so curiously removed from the strenuous and painful
experience of the hero, have the leisure and luxury to consume
stories as entertainment, the hero himself is constrained to treat
storytelling as a way of getting things done, a highly effective
tool among others. For him the story of his experience must be
the experience of story, and the experience of story, as it were,
from the helve end.

I FATUM, FAMA, INFANDUM

I have dwelt at such length on storytelling in the *Odyssey* because
it seems to me that Homer's triumphant harmonization of narrative and experience, his serene confidence in the instrumental
value of a story as a direct intervention in the affairs of men,
suggests a world not only foreign to Vergil's temperament, but
in all probability unavailable to any poet whose activity has become bound up with, to the point of being dependent on, the
technology of writing. If Homer's meticulously circumstantial
accounts of transitional procedures, the arming of a hero, for
instance, result in the kind of passage before which the modern

reader may at times feel something like Don Quixote's impatience as he listens to his squire's endless account of rowing a herd of goats across a river one by one,[3] they nevertheless suggest a way of thinking in which doing and telling are not entirely distinct. That secondary epic, and the *Aeneid* in particular, does not evince the same scrupulous concern may have more to do with the acquisition of a firm sense of this distinction than it has to do with some putative shift in stylistic sensibility or a modification in the canons of realism. And the acquisition of the distinction may by no means imply an unqualified gain for the poet; he may come to feel that he is no longer a participant in the affairs of men but a mere recorder of them. He may come to wonder about what he is doing by telling and how it can matter, about just what his intervention in the affairs of men, if any, can amount to. If, to borrow Shelley's ringing romantic phrase, poets are the unacknowledged legislators of the world, what do they legislate and why are they left unacknowledged?

That Homer's serene harmonization of telling and doing, of narration and experience, has undergone disruption and become the source of considerable anxiety by the time we get to Vergil is powerfully suggested by the narration within the narration in the *Aeneid*, the hero's recounting in Books 2 and 3 of the Fall of Troy and his subsequent wanderings. It is first of all striking that Aeneas begins his story by asserting that it is in fact unnarratable, unsayable, *infandum*:

> 'Infandum, regina, iubes renovare dolorem.'
>
> (2.3)

> "Sorrow too deep to tell, your majesty,
> You order me to feel and tell once more."
>
> (3–4)

The *Odyssey* contains nothing quite like this plangent cry.[4] Aeneas's adjective suggests his lingering and passionate involvement with his story, the kind of intense nostalgia that marks the hero's mood in much of the first half of the poem. The line is a signal example of what C. P. Segal has recently called the "participatory voice" of the *Aeneid*, "the voice of emotion, passion, feeling involvement in the striving and suffering of human beings," as opposed to the "authorial voice," which is "the voice of the omniscient narrator who controls the action."[5] Ever since the appearance of Adam Parry's influential "The Two Voices of Vergil's *Aeneid*,"[6] there has been a tendency to find some distinction in Vergil's poem like the one identified by Segal, with perhaps an accompanying tendency to favor the inner and private voice over the outer and public. I will refer on the one hand to "the discourse of fate," spoken by the god or those who possess a special relation to divinity, and on the other to plain and ordinary human discourse, that partial and often muddled account of things which it is the lot of most of us to produce most of the time.

That Aeneas should preface his own narration by identifying it as *infandum*, unsayable, is at once to put it into opposition to the discourse of fate, for from Vergil's point of view the sad events Aeneas's story contains are not that which is unsayable, but precisely that which has already been said, that which has well and truly happened, the discourse of *fatum*, the word derived, of course, like *infandum*, from the stem of the verb *fari*, to say. It is tempting to see in much of Aeneas's narration a latent protest against this discourse of fate, and perhaps in this juncture of *infandum* and *fatum* at the outset we strike a form of the recurrent Vergilian pathos repeatedly generated by the incommensurability of a man's will and his destiny. Aeneas's account of the Fall of Troy seems shadowed by subjunctives and "if only's," pervaded by an implicit *utinam*, as if to express the vain wish that these terrible events really could have happened in another way, if only

the Trojans had had their wits about them. As Aeneas says of the
warning of Laocoön,

> 'et, si fata deum, si mens non laeva fuisset,
> impulerat ferro Argolicas foedare latebras,
> Troiaque nunc staret, Priamique arx alta maneres.'
>
> (2.54–56)

> "If the gods' will had not been sinister,
> If our own minds had not been crazed,
> He would have made us foul that Argive den
> With bloody steel, and Troy would stand today—
> O citadel of Priam, towering still!"   (76–80)

And the protest against fate becomes explicit somewhat later when
Aeneas calls the treacherous Sinon "fatisque deum defensus ini-
quis" (2.257) ("favored / By what the gods unjustly had decreed"
[345]).

We are not perhaps meant to think of Aeneas as entirely aware
of this protest, but it may strike us that the narrative act itself
is somehow implicated in it and may itself be an attempt at
implication. For any narrative is implicitly a repetition, the re-
covering of ground already covered in experience.[7] Freud discusses
in *Beyond the Pleasure Principle* the notion that repetition is an
attempt at mastery,[8] and it may be that Vergil offers Aeneas's
narrative as a highly ambiguous attempt to master the past,
ambiguous because it seems to hover between an attempt on the
one hand to master the past by remembering it and thus to sever
the self definitively from it, and on the other to master it by
repeating it in a futile attempt to revise it, to rewrite the gloomy
decree of Necessity in a form more congenial to individual will.
Narration may in this sense be an attempt not to serve *fatum* but
to replace it.

We are a very long way, it would seem, from the world of

Odysseus and its nearly seamless transitions from narrative to experience, from telling to doing. For Aeneas cannot intervene in the decree of fate and never could, although the "if only's" of his narrative seem to indicate that he thinks that he might have been able to do so. Telling his story can only involve him in futile repetition, can only reveal to him his will to die, or, what is for Vergil very much the same thing, his will to give up. It is significant that at the end of Book 3 and thus at the end of his story, Aeneas calls the death of Anchises "my final sorrow . . . the goal / Of all my seafaring" (3.946–47) ("hic labor extremus, longarum haec meta viarum" [714]). Vergil surely had in mind here that a *meta*, a pyramidal column, may mark either the finish line of a race *or* a turning point within it. (Indeed, he uses the word in the latter sense in 5.129 when Aeneas declares a rock in mid-sea the turning point for the ship race.) What Aeneas seems to regard as an endgame is in fact a cardinal point, a pivot in the discourse of fate.

The narration of Aeneas does, of course, accomplish something, do something. But it is surely a salient difference between the embedded story of the *Odyssey* and the embedded story of the *Aeneid* that the former furthers and abets the larger poem in which it is embedded, while the latter very nearly succeeds in bringing its matrix to a premature and inappropriate ending. That Aeneas's tale becomes part of an elaborate erotic snare, party to an unwitting seduction, suggests that complicity of narrative in implication and contamination mentioned above. Partly through the medium of narration, Dido falls in love with a superseded Aeneas, a hero of the Fall of Troy, not with the Aeneas whose proper scenario is given in the discourse of fate. The effect of the tale on Dido is to afflict her with a repetitive obsession:

> nunc eadem labente die convivia quaerit,
> Iliacosque iterum demens audire labores

exposcit pendetque iterum narrantis ab ore.

(4.77–79)

When the day waned she wanted to repeat
The banquet as before, to hear once more
In her wild need the throes of Ilium,
And once more hung on the narrator's words.

(107–10)

And it is striking that the immediate price both Aeneas and Dido
must pay for succumbing to this erotic snare, for protesting in
all truth the discourse of *fatum*, what has been said, is the aban-
donment of the self not to that which is unsayable, *infandum*,
but to that which is all too readily sayable, to *fama*, to that which
is *being* said.

Vergil's Rumor, *Fama*, is suggestively a Titan, an anti-Olym-
pian, daughter of Earth and younger sister to Coeus and Ence-
ladus. Or rather, as Vergil puts it, *ut perhibent* (4.179), "as they
say," that is, "as rumor has it," Rumor is a Titan whom her
mother Earth bore to spite the Olympian gods. Vergil makes
Rumor's origins uncertain and problematic for the very good
reason that rumors are precisely those utterances whose origins
are unknown or radically in doubt: rumor is speech without
authority, a tangle of unauthorized versions (that is, versions
without an author), that network of incipient narratives that
spreads in any community of speakers and might best be considered as the narrative principle out of control. Vergil's name for
this strange creature, *Fama*, is a third in that complex of terms
deriving from the verb *fari: infandum*, the unsayable; *fatum*, that
which has been said; *fama*, that which is being said and is in this
context of dubious value.[9]

Fama is one of those words (and Latin has a particularly rich
store of them) that, like *sacer*, "sacred" and "accursed," or *altus*,
"high" and "deep," has antithetical meanings.[10] In the sense of

"repute," *fama* is interchangeably bad repute *and* good. It is clear, for instance, when Vergil says at the beginning of Book 7 that Caieta conferred "eternal fame" (*aeternam . . . famam* [2]) on Italian shores, he is using the word in the latter sense. This is *fama* brought under the control of *fatum* or within its purview. But in the fourth book the antithesis of *fama* really is *fatum*, that divine script from which Aeneas at Carthage so manifestly departs, delivering himself up, partly in the process of traversing a narrative of his own production, to the hum and buzz of unauthorized speech. At this the hero's nadir, a point at which the *Aeneid* itself verges on ending before it is well under way, Aeneas is in danger of becoming the fragmented hero of a disordered mass of gossip, a sample of which Vergil gives us in the chilling speech of the hard-boiled African king Iarbas, first in that series of *contemptores divum* in the *Aeneid* that culminates in Mezentius. As Iarbas says in what can scarcely be called his prayer to the father of gods and men (it is far more a threat),

> 'et nunc ille Paris cum semiviro comitatu,
> Maeonia mentum mitra crinemque madentem
> subnexus, rapto potitur: nos munera templis
> quippe tuis ferimus famamque fovemus inanem.'
>
> (4.215–18)

> "And now Sir Paris with his men, half-men,
> His chin and perfumed hair tied up
> In a Maeonian bonnet, takes possession.
> As for ourselves, here we are bringing gifts
> Into these shrines—supposedly your shrines—
> Hugging that empty fable."   (291–96)

In the hard world of Iarbas, Jupiter himself appears as a kind of unauthorized rumor, *famam . . . inanem*, as he says, an empty tale.

2 HOMER'S NEKUIA AND VERGIL'S DESCENT

That the act of narrating itself should have become for Vergil dark and problematic is altogether characteristic of the uncertain and often ambiguous world of the *Aeneid*, so different from what we might call, without undue sentimentalizing, the innocent clarity of the world of the *Odyssey*. When an act as apparently simple and natural in the circumstances as the hero's recounting of his experience before the monarch who has provided him a haven comes to have such catastrophic consequences, we may be sure that human discourse is no longer a simple and unproblematic phenomenon, that it has become darkly unwieldy with something like a life of its own quite independent of individual intention, a true "discourse of the Other" (I appropriate, of course, Jacques Lacan's famous, or perhaps notorious, definition of the unconscious), which is at once discourse about the Other and discourse originating in the Other. Language is no longer the field for mastery and the highly effective tool it is for Odysseus, which may help to explain the recurrent situation in the *Aeneid* where speech is refused or conversation abruptly broken off.[11] Repeating his sufferings in the form of a narrative cannot ensure the future for Aeneas, as it does for Odysseus; it can only enmesh him in the present and the past. It is certainly one of the functions of the great journey to the land of the dead in the sixth *Aeneid* to take the hero under divine auspices through a kind of ritual recapitulation of his experience and ultimately to free him from it. In this sense Vergil's descent to the underworld is a rewriting of the faulty narrative that the hero has produced for himself in Books 2 and 3 and suffered the consequences of in 4. It is preeminently an example of mortal discourse revised and corrected by the discourse of fate.[12]

It is also a spectacular rewriting of the eleventh *Odyssey*. By drawing on richly various elements of his literary heritage—not only Homer, but philosophical matter, procedures from the mystery religions, the legends of Hercules, folklore, and a great deal more—Vergil manages to give his descent to the underworld a prominence in his poem far greater than the analogous Homeric episode has in the *Odyssey*.[13] Homer's descent is likely to seem one more in the series of Odysseus's romantically exciting adventures. It is virtually unanticipated in the preceding narrative (it is first mentioned by Circe toward the end of the book that precedes it, 10.488–95), undertaken under her instruction, and partly recapitulated in the exchange Circe has with Odysseus upon his return (12.127–41: this is the warning about the cattle of Helios). The journey to the land of the dead by no means marks the culmination of Odysseus's wanderings, for he must still endure the Sirens, Scylla and Charybdis, the loss of his crew after the disastrous eating of the sun god's cattle, the bondage to Calypso, and the sojourn with the Phaeaecians. It is not that Homer's underworld episode is perfunctory—far from it—but it does tend to take its place among a series of equally vivid episodes in the wanderings, an ordeal that Odysseus by no means willingly endures as one further (and unforeseen) stage in the slow process of homecoming.

Vergil seems to have been attracted to the expansive effect, to the dilated episode carefully anticipated, richly developed, and repeatedly recalled. Of the books of the *Aeneid*, the second, the fourth, the fifth, the sixth, the eighth, and the twelfth are all of this type, while the third, often said to be the weakest in the *Aeneid*, with its *Odyssey*-like series of adventures, is arguably unlike anything else in the poem. Apparently Vergil did not write his best narrative poetry under the requirements of compression and speed. Homer could deal with an immense amount of material in short compass without seeming perfunctory. Vergil could not: evidently his forte was meticulously, expansively developed grandeur, and the sixth *Aeneid* may be the finest expression we have of the poetic gifts peculiar to him.

Vergil's descent is a Janus episode, at once a *cardo rerum* and a *limen*, looking backward and forward, the undoing of a private past and the creation of a public future. Nowhere are the "two voices" of the *Aeneid*, the one concerned with a personal past, the other with a glorious Roman future, more in evidence or more starkly juxtaposed, for the "rewriting" of the hero according to the terms of his destiny is very largely a matter of eliding human discourse and replacing it with the discourse of fate. A little more than half of Vergil's episode, up to the *arva ultima* (6.477–78; 641) and the end of the exchange with Deiphobus (547; 734), is devoted to a rehearsal of the past, but after Aeneas enters Elysium (637; 853) we are exclusively concerned with an exposition of the future. What lies in between these two transitional points is the Sybil's exposition of the punishments of Tartarus (548–627; 737–838) and the deposition of the golden bough on Proserpina's threshold (628–36; 841–52), the former a discursive passage dealing with the timeless figures of myth, the latter a ritual gesture to the meaning of which we shall have to return. Vergil may have found the two-fold structure suggested in *Odyssey* 11, where the hero encounters the shades of his fallen comrades and of his mother in addition to hearing prophecies of the future, but there is nothing like the evidence of careful patterning and suggestion that we find in *Aeneid* 6.

As R. S. Conway was perhaps the first modern commentator to observe, the order in which Aeneas encounters in the first half of his journey through the underworld the shades of those he has known in life is highly significant, for as he proceeds toward Elysium he encounters first Palinurus, only recently dead, then Dido, in her grave for what must be some months, and finally Deiphobus (whose name is mentioned in 2.310; 415), who has died at the hands of Menelaus and Ulysses on the night of Troy's fall some seven years before the death of Dido (6.509–34; 684–716).[14] The chiastic arrangement suggests not only a journey in space, but also a journey backward in time toward the Fall of Troy, the experience that Aeneas has attempted to repeat with a difference in his account of it to the Carthaginian queen. But this latter retrospective and regressive experience is ordered and guided by the discourse of fate as Aeneas's own narration is clearly not. It is a programmatic weaning of the hero from his past and is thus an inward experience quite unlike the experience of Odysseus in the land of the dead, which is for the most part a journey in search of practical wisdom pertinent to his homecoming.

As always, Homer's instrumental sense of narration is largely in evidence, a sense that is only vestigially present in the sixth *Aeneid*, and present only to be dismissed. Before the descent, when the Sybil has foretold new wars awaiting Aeneas in Italy, the hero responds to this factual prediction in barely three lines:

> 'non ulla laborum,
> o virgo, nova mi facies inopinave surgit;
> omnia praecepi atque animo mecum ante peregi.
> unum oro: quando hic inferni ianua regis
> dicitur et tenebrosa palus Acheronte refuso,
> ire ad conspectum cari genitoris et ora
> contingat.'   (103–9)

> "No novel kinds of hardship, no surprises,
> Loom ahead, Sister. I foresaw them all,
> Went through them in my mind. One thing I pray for:
> Since it is here they say one finds the gate
> Of the king of under world, the shadowy marsh
> That wells from Acheron, may I have leave
> To go to my dear father's side and see him."

                                                 (156–62)

The triple elision in line 105 bears eloquent witness to the haste with which Aeneas passes over the Sybil's prophecy and moves on to what is for him the central concern, the reunion with his father. Even here, Aeneas allows human discourse to supplant the discourse of fate.

If Aeneas's response to the Sybil's prophecy suggests his longing to be reunited with Anchises, his bearing during the journey itself suggests further that Aeneas thinks of this reunion as permanent and of Elysium as another of those idyllic settings like Carthage or the multiple sites at which he tries to found his city in Book 3, which are from the perspective of the discourse of fate digressions or traps. It is otherwise difficult to understand the emotional resonance of the anguished question Aeneas asks of his father when he is shown the shades by the Lethe preparing to return to the world above. The scene itself, with its river and grove and peaceful dwellings (6.703–5; 943–46), is hardly cause for shock or fear, and yet Vergil says of Aeneas "horrescit visu subito" (710) ("he shudders at the sudden vision"). The verb is peculiar enough in context that R. G. Austin suspected an unusual meaning: "Aeneas is startled with surprise. . . . an unusual use of the verb, but cf. Pacuvius, fr. 294 R, where it seems to mean a thrill of joy (the text is uncertain), *Pan. Lat.* 4 (10). 29.5 'cuius rei cum imaginem cepi, dicturus horresco,' where the context implies admiration."[5] But this seems at the very least to stretch a point. The problem is to construct a context where the usual meaning of *horresco* is appropriate. I propose that even though Vergil calls Aeneas *inscius* ("unknowing") at line 711, he imagines the truth about the nature of the scene dawning on the hero (the inchoative form of *horrescit*, literally, "he begins to shudder," may also suggest an incipient awareness), and that that truth is unpalatable. When Anchises makes the meaning of the scene explicit (713–15; 956–59), Aeneas's response is telling:

'o pater, anne aliquas ad caelum hinc ire putandum est
sublimis animas iterumque ad tarda reverti
corpora? quae lucis miseris tam dira cupido?'

(719–21)

> "Must we imagine,
> Father, there are souls that go from here
> Aloft to upper heaven, and once more
> Return to bodies' dead weight? The poor souls,
> How can they crave our daylight so?"

(965–69)

"Must we imagine": the periphrastic construction is strong, even stronger perhaps than the translation suggests, for it is impersonal—"Must it be thought?" This is the discourse of fate at its starkest, and it dispels at a stroke any hopes Aeneas may have had of a permanent reunion with his father in the Elysian Fields. Not for him the idyllic landscape, presided over, significantly, by the mythical bards Orpheus and Musaeus (645, 667; 864, 892): he too must endure a return to history and his high historical calling.

The crowd of souls on the banks of the Lethe recalls the other fluvial landscape in Vergil's underworld, the throng of recently dead awaiting passage over the Styx (6.305–16; 414–25). And here, again, Aeneas encounters the discourse of fate in particularly clear, and from the human perspective, even cruel, form. The shade of Palinurus, the helmsman struck overboard by the god Somnus in the preceding book (5.833–61; 1090–1126) during the voyage to Cumae, and denied passage to the realms of the dead because he remains unburied, accosts his former commander with what seems, after all, a modest request:

> 'quod te per caeli iucundum lumen et auras,
> per genitorem oro, per spes surgentis Iuli,
> eripe me his, invicte, malis: aut tu mihi terram

inice, namque potes, portusque require Velinos;
aut tu, si qua via est, si quam tibi diva creatrix
ostendit (neque enim, credo, sine numine divum
flumina tanta paras Stygiamque innare paludem),
da dextram misero et tecum me tolle per undas,
sedibus ut saltem placidis in morte quiescam.'

(6.363–71)

"By heaven's happy light
And the sweet air, I beg you, by your father,
And by your hopes of Iulus' rising star,
Deliver me from this captivity,
Unconquered friend! Throw earth on me—you can—
Put in to Velia port! Or if there be
Some way to do it, if your goddess mother
Shows a way—and I feel sure you pass
These streams and Stygian marsh by heaven's will—
Give this poor soul your hand, take me across,
Let me at least in death find quiet haven."

(490–500)

Although there is debate about the meaning of Palinurus's final line,[16] it seems reasonable to say that it implies a kind of muffled protest against his lot, that he has wandered restlessly for years in the world above, has paid the ultimate price, and has still not achieved peace, even in death. The implied protest may help explain the energy of the Sybil's rejoinder (Aeneas, whom Palinurus has addressed, is significantly overridden and not allowed to reply):

'unde haec, o Palinure, tibi tam dira cupido?
tu Stygias inhumatus aquas amnemque severum
Eumenidum aspicies, ripamve iniussus adibis?
desine fata deum flecti sperare precando.'

(373–76)

"From what source comes this craving, Palinurus?
Would you though still unburied see the Styx
And the grim river of the Eumenides,
Or even the river bank, without a summons?
Abandon hope by prayer to make the gods
Change their decrees."   (502–7)

The discourse of fate, what the Sibyl here calls *fata deum*, does not bend for mere human discourse (*precando*): what has been said has been said, and Palinurus (and by extension Aeneas, who has shortly before at line 332 been contemplating the *sortem . . . iniquam*, the "unjust lot," of the unburied) must accommodate himself to it.

That the Sibyl should call Palinurus's longing for rest a *dira cupido*, a "craving" or "dire longing," may strike us as excessive in context, accustomed as we are to regarding events from the ordinary human perspective. His prayer seems so natural and so modest given his circumstances. And yet the phrase *tam dira cupido* is precisely repeated (and in the identical position in the hexameter) during the other fluvial scene of Book 6 by Aeneas himself in his anguished question to his father: *quae lucis miseris tam dira cupido?* (721). It is surely significant that the Sybil uses the phrase to describe the human desire for rest, while Aeneas uses it to describe what seems to him an inhuman desire to return to labor and suffering when that rest has already been achieved. Nowhere perhaps are the divine and human perspectives so clearly opposed, and if the discourse of fate ultimately prevails (indeed *must* prevail in the larger scheme of the *Aeneid*—what is a matter of prophecy for the hero is a matter of history for the reader),[17] it is characteristic of Vergil that he never forgets the pathos and loss involved when the discourse of fate overrides, as it must, the compellingly human voices that quietly speak in every corner of his poem. We recall the Sybil's often quoted words in reply to Aeneas's request to visit the land of the dead:

> 'sate sanguine divum,
> Tros Anchisiade, facilis descensus Averno:
> noctes atque dies patet atri ianua Ditis;
> sed revocare gradum superasque evadere ad auras,
> hoc opus, hic labor est.'   (6.125–29)

> "Offspring
> Of gods by blood, Trojan Anchises' son,
> The way downward is easy from Avernus.
> Black Dis's door stands open night and day.
> But to retrace your steps to heaven's air,
> There is the trouble, there is the toil."

> (185–90)

It is perhaps only in Elysium that the full purport of the Sybil's words is revealed to the hero. The toil and trouble of the return have more to do with the inward task of submitting to the discourse of fate than they have to do with any physical labor of ascending.

3 AENEAS AND THE FERRYMAN

It is evident that Vergil was far more concerned than the Homer of the *Odyssey* with the education of his hero in the broadest sense. The obstacles that thwart the Homeric hero's homecoming are uniformly external, imposed by a world that is by turns too hostile and too loving. Odysseus must acquire information and deploy techniques, but the *Odyssey* is concerned little, if at all, with his development: it is instead the story of his progress.

Some such distinction is pertinent to the *Aeneid* at all levels, for again it is only when we can think of development, of differences between one time and another succeeding it, that the idea of history intervenes. And the *Aeneid* is preeminently concerned with the historical dimension of things, with the history of the hero (and not just with his story), with the history of the collective that the hero will found, and finally with the history of the epic genre in which the deeds of hero and collective are recorded. These various histories are, of course, closely interwoven and thoroughly interdependent; to separate them at all can only be justified in the name of convenience.[18]

It can scarcely be doubted by now—it has been intimated since ancient times—that Vergil offers in the *Aeneid* a radically new concept of heroism based on the peculiarly Roman virtue of *pietas*, that complex of attitudes toward one's parents and family, toward one's country, and toward one's gods that can only be inadequately translated as "respect," or perhaps "respectful reverence." That Vergilian *pietas* involves a large measure of renunciation, a placing of the self in the hands of higher powers and at the disposal of transpersonal ideals, may help to account for the enormous appeal of the *Aeneid* in the Christian Middle Ages. By making *pietas* the center of his hero's character, Vergil founded a heroic code based on service and dedication rather than on self-assertion, and he succeeded so well that many have since denied Aeneas heroic stature.[19]

What must always be stressed is the self-conscious nature of Vergil's revision. The new code does not come easily or naturally to Aeneas, trained up as he has been in something like the values of a Bronze Age warrior. By his own account, his first impulse on discovering that his city is in flames is to seize arms and futilely, even suicidally, enter the fray, for arms are, so to speak, the only language he knows. Aeneas at the Fall of Troy must be told repeatedly to flee rather than to stand and fight a hopeless battle, first by the shade of Hector (2.289–95; 385–97), then by

Panthus, the priest of Apollo (324–35; 435–49), next by his divine mother (594–620; 780–812), and finally by the shade of Creusa (776–89; 1007–25). There can be no question of the new code being present in the hero from the beginning, and it may be doubted that its traces are completely effaced by the end of the poem in the hero or in anyone else, including the reader.[20] By dramatizing such tensions Vergil reveals his awareness of the Homeric heritage and indeed his awareness of his own position in relation to the Homeric poems, the presence of which in the *Aeneid* as the most important intertext is part of the poem's meaning.

Vergil's allusive technique is extraordinarily complex: it may be a question of the refitting of a single Homeric line, the refashioning of an entire speech, the close imitation of an episode, large or small, or a less specific inclusion of the *kind* of episode found in Homer or more broadly in the Greek tradition.[21] Let us consider two examples, one of the second type, briefly, and one of the last type at somewhat greater length.

Aeneas's speech to his storm-wracked companions after his landing at Carthage in the first book may serve as an example of the way Vergil imitates a Homeric speech but changes it profoundly through context and environment:

'O socii (neque enim ignari sumus ante malorum),
o passi graviora, dabit deus his quoque finem.
vos et Scyllaeam rabiem penitusque sonantis
accestis scopulos, vos et Cyclopia saxa
experti: revocate animos maestumque timorem
mittite; forsan et haec olim meminisse iuvabit.
per varios casus, per tot discrimina rerum
tendimus in Latium, sedes ubi fata quietas
ostendunt; illic fas regna resurgere Troiae.

durate, et vosmet rebus servate secundis.'
  Talia voce refert curisque ingentibus aeger
spem vultu simulat, premit altum corde dolorem.

(1.198–209)

            "Friends and companions,
Have we not known hard hours before this?
My men, who have endured still greater dangers,
God will grant us an end to these as well.
You sailed by Scylla's rage, her booming crags,
You saw the Cyclops' boulders. Now call back
Your courage, and have done with fear and sorrow.
Some day, perhaps, remembering even this
Will be a pleasure. Through diversities
Of luck, and through so many challenges,
We hold our course for Latium, where the Fates
Hold out a settlement and rest for us.
Troy's kingdom there shall rise again. Be patient:
Save yourselves for more auspicious days."

So ran the speech. Burdened and sick at heart,
He feigned hope in his look, and inwardly
Contained his anguish.   (270–86)

The speech is in part a rather close imitation of Odysseus's exhortation to his men as they prepare to pass Scylla and Charybdis
(12.208–21), and yet its meaning and purport are utterly different. "Dear friends," the crafty Odysseus begins,

        "surely we are not unlearned in evils,
  this is no greater evil now than it was when the Cyclops
  had us cooped in his hollow cave by force and violence.
  But even there, by my courage and counsel and my
      intelligence,

we escaped away. I think that this will be remembered
someday too. Then do as I say, let us all be won over."

                                        (12.208–13)

This has its effect; the men fall to the oars. But it succeeds as
much for what Odysseus prudently does *not* mention. 'So I spoke,'
he says,

> 'and they quickly obeyed my words. I had not
> spoken yet of Skylla, a plague that could not be dealt with,
> for fear my companions might be terrified and give over
> their rowing, and take cover inside the ship.'   (222–25)

Aeneas, like Odysseus, holds something back, but it is not
the precise knowledge of danger (he has no such precise knowledge
and would not suppress it if he did), but the fact of his own
uncertainty and grief. This is not the skillful rhetorician, proud
of his abilities; it is the man struck by real doubt trying to put
a good face on things for the common welfare, a man not so
much moved by heroic pride (there is no question of Aeneas's
being ashamed of his feelings) as by a sense of duty in the face
of the unknown. And it is, for all the sincere attempt at encouragement, an ambiguous and uncertain speech. It contains
one of the most often quoted lines in the poem, one that has
become a virtual tag: "forsan et haec olim meminisse iuvabit"
("Some day, perhaps, remembering even this / Will be a pleasure"). The line has become so familiar that we may miss the fact
that it admits of a double meaning. Aeneas means, of course,
that better times are coming, when they will be able to look
back at their toils with detachment and understanding. But he
implies, without perhaps quite meaning to, something rather
different, that perhaps so much worse is on the way that even
this, bad as it is, will seem preferable.

The human uncertainty of the speech and its crucial difference from the confidently duplicitous speech of Odysseus are further emphasized by its occurrence immediately before the divine colloquy between Venus and Jupiter (1.223–96; 304–98), where the father of gods and men tells the secrets of fate ("volvens fatorum arcana movebo" [262]) and soothes the ruffled feelings of his daughter. We have just left Aeneas in deep mourning for his missing companions (some of whom will reappear at Carthage; the point is that Aeneas cannot know this), when the perspective shifts abruptly to Jupiter as he looks below and comprehends all things. The contrast with the muddled and uncertain comprehension of Aeneas is surely pointed, and the difference between the speech of the god and the speech of the man is an example as clear as we could wish of the contrast between the discourse of fate and ordinary human discourse. The *Odyssey* simply does not deal with contrasts of this depth, which is not to say that it is inferior (Vergil implies nothing of the sort here), but only to say that it treats a very different range of human experience.

Aeneas's speech must suffice as an example of one way Vergil deploys a specific Homeric intertext to foreground the unique character of his own poem and hero. Never have we to do with passive imitation merely, for the presence of the Homeric texts within the text of the *Aeneid* is part of the meaning of the poem, part of the way it achieves meaning. And so it is with a somewhat broader and less focused effect characteristic of Vergil, the introduction, for instance, of Homeric warriors in a very un-Homeric light (the thoroughly cruel Ulysses of the second book, the representation of Achilles in the frieze on the temple at Carthage selling the corpse of Hector for gold [1.484; 659–60]), or the importation of material not specifically Homeric from Greek legend and myth.

It is to the latter technique that we now turn, and specifically to the encounter with Charon, the traditional ferryman of the river Styx, in the sixth book. Though Charon is post-Homeric,[22]

Vergil characterizes him as thoroughly archaic, and for all the terrifying impressiveness of the figure, there is a shabby, threadbare quality about him that suggests the impotence of his authority side by side with the indications of his power:

> turbidus hic caeno vastaque voragine gurges
> aestuat atque omnem Cocyto eructat harenam.
> portitor has horrendus aquas et flumina servat
> terribili squalore Charon, cui plurima mento
> canities inculta iacet, stant lumina flamma,
> sordidus ex umeris nodo dependet amictus.
> ipse ratem conto subigit velisque ministrat
> et ferruginea subvectat corpora cumba,
> iam senior, sed cruda deo viridisque senectus.
>
> 　　　　　　　　(6.296–304)

> 　　　　Thick with mud,
> A whirlpool out of a vast abyss
> Boils up and belches all the silt it carries
> Into Cocytus. Here the ferryman,
> A figure of fright, keeper of waters and streams,
> Is Charon, foul and terrible, his beard
> Grown wild and hoar, his staring eyes all flame,
> His sordid cloak hung from a shoulder knot.
> Alone he poles his craft and trims the sails
> And in his rusty hull ferries the dead,
> Old now—but old age in the gods is green.
>
> 　　　　　　　　(404–14)

There is something distinctly amusing in the fact that this ragged figure with his leaky boat should be so officious, should sound for all the world like a touchy customs officer. And yet his previous experience of visiting heroes has led him to expect disruptive exploits of derring-do. His challenge, flung at Aeneas and the Sybil from the middle of the river (Charon wants it

immediately known that he has spotted the potentially trouble-
some living man in the crowd of shades), is both funny and
revealing:

> 'quisquis es, armatus qui nostra ad flumina tendis,
> fare age quid venias iam istinc, et comprime gressum.
> umbrarum hic locus est, somni noctisque soporae:
> corpora viva nefas Stygia vectare carina.
> nec vero Alciden me sum laetatus euntem
> accepisse lacu, nec Thesea Pirithoumque,
> dis quamquam geniti atque invicti viribus essent.
> Tartareum ille manu custodem in vincla petivit
> ipsius a solio regis traxitque trementem;
> hi dominam Ditis thalamo deducere adorti.'
>
> (6.388–97)

> "Who are you
> In armor, visiting our rivers? Speak
> From where you are, stop there, say why you come.
> This is the region of the Shades, and Sleep,
> And drowsy Night. It breaks eternal law
> For the Stygian craft to carry living bodies.
> Never did I rejoice, I tell you, letting
> Alcides cross, or Theseus and Pirithous,
> Demigods by paternity though they were,
> Invincible in power. One forced in chains
> From the king's own seat the watchdog of the dead
> And dragged him away trembling. The other two
> Were bent on carrying our lady off
> From Dis's chamber."   (520–33)

What Charon expects from Aeneas, whom he knows as yet only
as a man in armor, is a piratical raid of the kind the Greek heroes
have attempted, a dog- or queen-napping. He is completely unprepared for the hero new-style, who comes on a pious pilgrimage

to his father and not in quest of spoil. The Sybil's reply, which betrays a wonderful impatience with Charon's resistance, attempts to set the ferryman straight about this distinction, and in no uncertain terms:

'nullae hic insidiae tales (absiste moveri),
nec vim tela ferunt; licet ingens ianitor antro
aeternum latrans exsanguis terreat umbras,
casta licet patrui servet Proserpina limen.
Troius Aeneas, pietate insignis et armis,
ad genitorem imas Erebi descendit ad umbras.
si te nulla movet tantae pietatis imago,
at ramum hunc' (aperit ramum qui veste latebat)
'agnoscas.' tumida ex ira tum corda residunt.

(399–407)

        "Here are no such plots,
So fret no more. These weapons threaten nothing.
Let the great watchdog at the door howl on
Forever terrifying the bloodless shades.
Let chaste Proserpina remain at home
In her uncle's house. The man of Troy, Aeneas,
Remarkable for loyalty, great in arms,
Goes through the deepest shades of Erebus
To see his father.
        If the very image
Of so much goodness moves you not at all,
Here is a bough"—at this she showed the bough
That had been hidden, held beneath her dress—
"You'll recognize it."
        Then his heart, puffed up
With rage, subsided.   (537–52)

There are several aspects of the Sybil's rejoinder that are noteworthy, and not the least of these is her way of referring to Aeneas as "Troius Aeneas, pietate insignis et armis," where pride of place is clearly given to *pietas*, the inner value of reverence and respect, over whatever martial prowess is implied in the word *armis*. The Sybil stresses the hero's Trojan lineage and implies that Charon need not fear from Aeneas what he has had every reason to fear from the Greeks who have made the descent to the land of the dead. It is interesting in this context that Charon's challenge has echoed in one significant aspect the Sybil's response to Aeneas's initial request in the Cumaean cave to visit his father in the land of the dead. In his challenge Charon describes the heroes who have preceded Aeneas as "dis quamquam geniti atque invicti viribus" (6.394) ("Demigods by paternity . . . / Invincible in power"). Of those few who have made the descent *and* returned, the Sybil has said,

> 'pauci, quos aequus amavit
> Iuppiter aut ardens evexit ad aethera virtus,
> dis geniti potuere.'   (129–31)

"A few, born of the gods, whom just Jupiter loved or whom ardent virtue bore aloft to the heavens, have been able."[23] It is surely significant in context that where Charon speaks of *vires* the Sybil speaks of *virtus*, for the distinction indicates the gap between physical prowess with its accompanying violence (*vis* is, of course, the etymon of our word "violence") and something far closer to what we mean by virtue in the ethical sense.

Charon quite naturally concentrates on *vires*, as he nervously eyes a living man in armor: he knows all too well the consequences of admitting such a figure to his domains. This is perhaps why the Sybil insists on what we can only understand as the symbolic character of the weapons Aeneas bears: "nec vim tela ferunt (6.399), she asserts ("These weapons threaten nothing" [538]). The assertion is particularly striking, because at the entrance to the underworld, shortly before encountering Charon, the Sybil

has exhorted Aeneas to draw his sword, as if he might have some
occasion to use it:

> 'tuque invade viam vaginaque eripe ferrum:
> nunc animis opus, Aenea, nunc pectore firmo.'
>
> (260–61)

> "But you, Aeneas,
> Enter the path here, and unsheathe your sword.
> There's need of gall and resolution now."
>
> (358–60)

But when Aeneas encounters the throng of Gorgons and Harpies,
Scyllas and Centaurs within the vestibule of the underworld and
naturally looks to his sword to defend himself (heroism old style
is a habit), the Sybil specifically restrains him:

> corripit hic subita trepidus formidine ferrum
> Aeneas strictamque aciem venientibus offert,
> et ni docta comes tenuis sine corpore vitas
> admoneat volitare cava sub imagine formae,
> inruat et frustra ferro diverberet umbras.
>
> (290–94)

> Here, swept by sudden fear, drawing his sword,
> Aeneas stood on guard with naked edge
> Against them as they came. If his companion,
> Knowing the truth, had not admonished him
> How faint these lives were—empty images
> Hovering bodiless—he had attacked
> And cut his way through phantoms, empty air.
>
> (396–402)

Nec vim tela ferunt, in fact: this weapon *has* no force.[24] Aeneas's
arms are evidently the sign of his heroic lineage (and so Charon
nervously reads them), but they are in the underworld merely

the sign of heroic status and not the traditional implements of the traditional hero.

We may think of the figure of Charon as a kind of metonymy for what is from the point of view of the new-style heroism an entire outmoded tradition. It is in relation to Charon and his archaic expectations that Vergil succeeds in foregrounding his own hero and the new ethic which that hero is in the process of acquiring in his underworld journey. " 'Licet ingens ianitor antro / aeternum latrans exsanguis terreat umbras' " (6.399–400), the Sybil says in her impatient rejoinder to the ferryman ("Let the great watchdog at the door howl on / Forever terrifying the bloodless shades" [539–40]). The adverbial *aeternum* in emphatic position suggests something like a historyless world in which these mythical figures will continue forever their repetitive repertoire.[25] The Sybil suggests that whatever they do will not be of much consequence to the new-style hero whose destiny is eschatological and historical, not mythical and timeless. Charon collapses at the mere sight of the golden bough. Cerberus succumbs abruptly to the lump of drugged meal the Sybil summarily tosses him (419–23; 566–71).[26] Two kinds of representation, the mythical and the historical, collide, and Vergil leaves us in no doubt as to which is the more pertinent to the *Aeneid* as a whole.

What *is* of avail in the underworld, if not the hero's traditional arms, is the golden bough.[27] It too, of course, is a sign or a symbol, though a symbol of *what* remains very much in question. In any case, the bough is significantly opposed to the sword in the Sybil's instructions toward the beginning of Book 6 about procuring it:

> 'namque ipse volens facilisque sequetur,
> si te fata vocant; aliter non viribus ullis
> vincere nec duro poteris convellere ferro.'
>
> (146–48)

"It will come willingly,
Easily, if you are called by fate.
If not, with all your strength you cannot conquer it,
Cannot lop it off with a sword's edge." (214–17)

Neither strength—*vires*—nor steel: the bough has nothing to do with physical prowess; you cannot simply hack it away with an axe. It requires not the man of *vires*, but the man of *virtus*. The two terms are related, but the latter is surely the one that points to the inner values, to the *pietas*, with which the sixth book is so largely concerned.

Virtus and *vires*, or *virtus* as opposed to *vires*. Both words contain the Latin *vir*, "man," the word so prominently on display in the first line of the poem, *Arma virumque cano*. By the end of Book 6 we know what man Vergil sings, or rather what *kind* of man he sings. The old heroes, the memory of whom makes Charon so nervous, the men of *vires*, have made a raid on the realms of the dead, descended in search of spoil. Their purpose has been to wrest something from death's kingdom, and perhaps in so doing they have attempted to assert their superiority over death itself. Aeneas, on the other hand, the man of *virtus*, gets his spoil, if it really is that, in the world above. He bears the golden bough as tribute to Proserpina, the queen of the dead; he has no other designs upon her. It is perhaps not too much to see in the gesture of leaving the bough for Proserpina a token of the hero's assent to his own death, his dedication of himself to history and the future, to *famamque et fata nepotum* (8.731) ("the destined acts / And fame of his descendants" [991–92]). To accept one's *own* mortality—that is in large measure what it means to be a man of *virtus*.

But acquiescence in his own mortality is a particularly difficult problem for Aeneas, because it entails something quite different from the sleep of death, a respite for the weary man buffeted by fortune. It is mortality in and for history, not a personal release. And with history we are returned to the realm of the inescapably problematic. We have already seen what Aeneas's question to Anchises about the souls assembled at the Lethe implies about his state of mind; he is vouchsafed no happy idyll in the never-never land of Elysium, for like the assembled souls, he too must return to a historical calling, to ordinary human discourse with all its complexities and ambiguities. And even as Anchises calls the roll of future Roman worthies, we catch again some whispering of the uncertainties, the fundamentally problematic character of human discourse:

> 'vis et Tarquinios reges animamque superbam
> ultoris Bruti, fascisque videre receptos?
> consulis imperium hic primus saevasque securis
> accipiet, natosque pater nova bella moventis
> ad poenam pulchra pro libertate vocabit.
> infelix! utcumque ferent ea facta minores:
> vincet amor patriae laudumque immensa cupido.'
>
> (6.817–23)

> "Do you care to see now, too, the Tarquin kings
> And the proud soul of the avenger, Brutus,
> By whom the bundled *fasces* are regained?
> Consular power will first be his, and his
> The pitiless axes. When his own two sons
> Plot war against the city, he will call
> For the death penalty in freedom's name—
> Unhappy man, no matter how posterity
> May see these matters. Love of the fatherland
> Will sway him—and unmeasured lust for fame."
>
> (1099–1108)

It is extraordinarily difficult to form a univocal attitude toward the figure of Lucius Junius Brutus: he is at once a hero of the early republic and a "proud soul" (*superbam*) in search of personal reknown (*laudumque immensa cupido*). If his pious dedication to the republic is reason for admiration, it is achieved only at the expense of what is for Vergil the heart and foundation of any political order, republican or otherwise, the relation between father and son. And if to dedicate the self to the state before all other things is to follow the discourse of fate, to seek reknown is at the same time to dedicate the self to human discourse, to what people will say: it is, in short, to reenter the ambiguous arena of *fama*. In the very midst of Anchises' presentation we are reminded not of the orderly progression of fate, but of experience as it is given to us with all its contradictions, complexities, and undecidable choices.

4 THE DISCOURSE OF FATE

As the discourse of fate the sixth *Aeneid* is perhaps the most flawless art of which Vergil was capable, and it clearly enjoins flawlessness on the hero. Yet Aeneas must return to what he himself calls *tarda . . . corpora* (6.720–21), in Fitzgerald's apt phrase, "to bodies' dead weight," to experience in all its recalcitrance, not to a vision of experience ordered and purified by the discourse of fate. In this conflict we can glimpse something of the problem posed by the last half of the poem, perhaps even something of Vergil the poet's awareness of the problem of imposing form and order on experience. Aeneas leaves the world below and enters the experiential world of Italy through the gate of false dreams (898; 1216–18). The meaning of the passage has been debated since ancient times and will probably always be debated.[28] Let us simply note that there is a gate of true dreams as well, and that it is made of horn, a rough substance not suited to the finest works of art, while the gate of false dreams is of polished ivory, *perfecta* Vergil calls it (895) ("finished," "perfected"). Perhaps the man issuing from the polished gate is in some sense false just because he is *not* really perfected, because he is, after all, still human, still burdened with the body's dead weight. From the perspective of the discourse of fate he is false, even if from the human perspective he is, in all his fallibility, all too true. In a way the Homeric heroes can never quite be, he is an image of the reader.

Many critical accounts of the *Aeneid*, and many of them very good, point out the symmetries of Vergil's poem, its balanced and orderly architecture. Thus Brooks Otis speaks of "the plan of the whole poem: six books depicting the inner struggle for *pietas*; six depicting the triumph of *pietas* over the *impii*."[29] We may agree with the first half of this formulation while pausing to wonder a little about the second. For if the first half of the poem has led us to expect some satisfying symmetries, if it has promised some consummations to be discharged in the second, we are often disappointed, and perhaps our disappointment is part of Vergil's meaning. The Sybil speaks, for example, of a second Achilles awaiting Aeneas in Latium (6.89–90; 135–36). This must be Turnus, and we may come to expect in the second half of the poem one of those neat reversals where the slayer is finally slain in his turn. That tidy resolution would have the perfection of ivory, but it is scarcely what we get. It is as difficult to adopt a univocal attitude toward Turnus as it is to adopt one toward the visionary figure of Junius Brutus, and it is difficult, I think, because Vergil has purposely made it so. Turnus is no villain pure and simple; he is a human being, with all the attendant baggage of feeling, confusion, and uncertainty that goes with that status. Turnus has his Achillean moments, to be sure, as when in Book 9 he slays Pandarus within the Trojan camp and contemptuously tells him to bear the message to Priam, " 'hic etiam inventum Priamo narrabis Achillem' " (9.742) ("You will be telling Priam / Achilles has been found again, and here"

[1031–32]).[30] But it is important to recognize that they are only moments, and that they scarcely correspond to the complete impression of Turnus Vergil has given us, to his youth and vitality, to his fears and self-doubts, to the humanly forgetful Turnus of that moment in Book 12 (735–37; 994–97), which might be funny if the stakes were not so terribly high, who discovers he has left his good sword at home. Experience, Vergil reminds us, does not deal in symmetry, in the perfection of ivory, but in the roughness of horn. We are asked, after all, to comprehend Turnus not only as a furious Achilles, but also as a suppliant, in Anchises' words in 6.853; 1154, as a proud man to be battled down, but also as a conquered man to be spared. It seems to me that we can neither forgive Aeneas for killing Turnus in the end nor blame him. Vergil has given us a situation that is simply undecidable. It is certainly not a matter of establishing Turnus's guilt or his inadequacy. That pseudo-Aristotelian approach has consistently failed to provide any adequate explanation of the final scene of the poem.

We have been told repeatedly that the *Aeneid* as we have it is unfinished, that at the time of his death Vergil was planning extensive revisions. We will never know just what he proposed to change or augment or reduce. Let me speculate in conclusion, however, that, whatever Vergil's plans, the ending of the poem as we have it is the one he intended. It is *not* a conclusion properly speaking, and that is part of the point. If the *Aeneid* really were the fawning encomium of Augustus Caesar that some have said it is, the argument that it is unfinished might have greater force: it *does* seem an odd way to praise Augustus to leave his putative ancestor and fictional analogue killing a suppliant in a moment of vengeful rage. The second Achilles Aeneas confronts in Latium is ultimately a possibility in himself, in Caesar Augustus, in all of us, far more than a specific character. If we assume on the other hand that the *Aeneid* is not an encomium of Augustus but a prompting, a warning, an indication of the open-ended and on-going status of the project of founding Rome, the ending as we have it begins to make a kind of painful sense.

As indicated above, the *Aeneid* seems at certain crucial points to court premature endings. Perhaps Aeneas's narration at Carthage and his subsequent sojourn there are the clearest examples of such courting, but they are by no means the only ones. Book 3, the wanderings, furnishes a string of such false endings, blind alleys, dead ends, abortive attempts to found a city in the wrong place, and a remarkable visit with Helenus and Andromache at Buthrotum (294–505; 396–670), an episode that characterizes what can only be called the pathos of repetition. The miniature simulacrum of Troy that they have built, with its dry brook named Xanthus and its empty tomb commemorating Hector, may be touching in its way, but it exemplifies the sterility of the attempt to live in the past. It reminds us that the will to repeat is internal to Aeneas, and that one of the signal differences between him and his counterpart in the *Odyssey* is that the impulse to come to a stop emerges from within him and is by and large not something imposed on him by the world in which he moves. What Aeneas accomplishes in his final act is a vendetta. There is no gainsaying that:

> 'tune hinc spoliis indute meorum
> eripiare mihi? Pallas te hoc vulnere, Pallas
> immolat et poenam scelerato ex sanguine sumit.'
> hoc dicens ferrum adverso sub pectore condit
> fervidus. ast illi solvuntur frigore membra
> vitaque cum gemitu fugit indignata sub umbras.
>
> (12.947–52)

"You in your plunder, torn from one of mine,
Shall I be robbed of you? This wound will come

From Pallas: Pallas makes this offering
And from your criminal blood exacts his due."

He sank his blade in fury in Turnus' chest.
Then all the body slackened in death's chill,
And with a groan for that indignity
His spirit fled into the gloom below.

(1291–98)

This is the end (if not the conclusion) of the poem. We are reminded that revenge is the compulsion to repeat in its clearest and most dreadful form.

It seems unlikely that, given his concern with premature endings, Vergil could have been entirely unaware of the fact that closure constitutes a problem for the narrative poet as well as for his hero, and the very open-endedness of the *Aeneid* as we have it speaks to this problem. If the poem ends with an act of repetition on the part of the hero, a wrathful vengeance that is surely intended to remind us of the Achilles of the *Iliad*, it does not follow that the poet himself has suddenly forgotten the problem of repetition and premature endings. In describing the act of Aeneas plunging his sword into the breast of Turnus, Vergil uses a locution that may appear to be merely a mild and insignificant catachresis: "hoc dicens ferrum adverso sub pectore condit / fervidus" (950–51) ("He sank his blade in fury in Turnus' chest" [1295]; more literally, of course, "He hides his blade in fury in Turnus' chest"). The verb *condere* is suggestive here, because we surely recall its alternative and perhaps antithetical meaning "to found," the way, for instance, it is used at the very beginning of the poem, "dum conderet urbem" (1.5) ("till he could found a city" [10]), "tantae molis erat Romanam condere gentem" (33) ("so hard and huge / A task it was to found the Roman people" [43–44]).[31] Aeneas may risk hiding or doing away with a good

deal more than his sword and Turnus in his final act, for surely
you do not found the kind of city Vergil has in mind by hiding
your sword in the breast of a suppliant. The name *Latium*, as
Vergil tells us in his eighth book (319–23; 423–29), derives from
the Latin verb *latere*, "to lie hidden," and whether this is a true
or false etymology matters little. The preeminent city of the
region may still in a sense be a hiding place and thus a hidden
place. The Rome Vergil speaks of most eloquently is not the
structure of dressed stone that Augustus could see all about him,
but a dream of justice and order that must be founded, refounded,
found again and again. Latium is still a hidden place, and Vergil
did not write the *Aeneid* to congratulate Caesar Augustus on the
occasion of his having found it. That would have been to end
prematurely indeed. He wrote the *Aeneid* lest Caesar should cease
trying to find it and found it.

II

Dante: Language and History

IT is a curious accident of literary history that in spite of the fact that Dante's *Commedia* internalizes much of the text of the *Aeneid* and the author of that text as well, it more closely resembles in certain stylistic and mimetic features the Homeric poems, which Dante never read, than it does the *Aeneid*, which it is clear he read with the strictest attention and may have even known by heart. There is little in the *Commedia* to remind us of the Vergilian soft focus, the crucial open-endedness remarked in the conclusion of the preceding chapter, and if there is uncertainty, it is a question of the uncertainty of Dante the pilgrim, the bewildered figure of the first two cantos of the poem, who is taken through the underworld precisely to rid him of his uncertainty, to educate him in the plan of Providence. Dante the poet, on the other hand, the narrative voice of the *Commedia* and the fully educated product of the otherworld journey, speaks with a firm authority that is in significant contrast to the hesitant and tentative gropings of his earlier self. Something like Homer's celebrated objectivity, the clarity and firmness of that vision which Homer attributes to the daughters of Mnemosyne, is part of Dante's *Commedia* as well. There is no room in Dante's poem for the qualifying phrases, the disclaimers like *si credere dignum est* or *ut fama est* which occur so often in the narrative voice of the *Aeneid*.

We have already noted that Aeneas leaves Vergil's underworld through the gate of false dreams and that in so doing he may become something like a false dream himself. It is in any case a fact that the underworld is not something the hero can get free of simply by passing through. The second half of the *Aeneid* is full of infernal rumblings, fury, and the stirrings of demonic powers. Early in the seventh book Juno conjures the dreadful Fury Allecto from the world below (323ff.; 442ff.) and sets the tone for much that is to follow. And at the very end of the poem Jupiter sends down one of the *Dirae*, who sinisterly enough have their place by the very throne of the father of gods and men (12.849; 1111), to serve notice on Turnus of the grim fate that awaits him. The forces of darkness are scarcely laid to rest in the *Aeneid*, and in the final instance they come from their place by the king of the gods himself. It is no coincidence that the last word of the *Aeneid* is *umbras*.

It may have been just such qualities of the *Aeneid*, its crucial vagueness, its open-endedness, its lack of a triumphant resolution, that attracted Dante to it, at least when he came to consider the project of his massive poem. Whether or not he knew the ancient accounts of Vergil's supposed dissatisfaction with his poem, those dramatic stories of his death-bed demand that the *Aeneid* be burnt, and whether or not he believed them if he did know them, are questions that need not finally be settled. The *Aeneid is* unfinished in the only way that really mattered to Dante in that it points to an idea at which it never really arrives, the idea of a perfectly harmonious, perfectly unified earthly city, the cultural ideal that is implicit in that thing Vergil calls *Roma*, and an idea so central to his vision, so closely associated with him in later times, that it is tempting to think that both Vergil and Dante must have noticed that its name is an anagram of one of Vergil's own names, Maro. The finished artifact, in the way that it encloses its predecessors, may well appear to close a tradition, while the unfinished artifact, in its very open-endedness, seems to create a future, to keep a space open for further history. It may well have been those empty spaces in the *Aeneid*, those points where there is a sudden loss of definition and focus, that drew Dante into it and finally beyond it.

Dante worked in what we might call a bibliocentric culture, a culture that accorded centrality and absolute authority to Scripture, while Vergil had no privileged text, but rather a mass of legend, folklore, myth, and the poetry of his predecessors, no one of whom, with the possible exception of Homer, had any claim to authority over the others. Vergil had to create an authoritative myth, where we might say, without for a minute disparaging or reducing his achievement, Dante had only to gloss one, to write his poem in the margin of the book he thought of as God's writing. Dante's situation in history is almost bound to produce writing of a certain clarity and firmness.

I THE *Commedia* AND THE CLASSICAL TRADITION

"The fiction of the *Divine Comedy* is that it is not fiction," C. S. Singleton has remarked.[1] The justice of this observation will be evident to anyone who has pondered Dante's massive poem as the record of an experience with its enormous diversity and wealth of detail, rendered real and present by the author's almost preternatural sensitivity to the shapes and attitudes of his world. Yet we must be exceedingly careful with such a formulation, lest it betray us into admitting Dante to the company of realists and naturalists, making of him a kind of Victorian novelist in *terza rima*. For the subject matter of the *Commedia* is never very close to what Francis Fergusson, speaking of nineteenth-century drama, calls a "pidgin-English of the imagination,"[2] but is rather always in touch with the fantastic, the monstrous, and the grotesque, those forms and images that we have become accustomed to calling "mythic." That Dante treated these matters as if they existed and eschewed the Vergilian device of calling them into question, so that constantly in his poem myth rubs elbows with legend and history and history with the contemporary, is part of an effort everywhere evident to secure the illusion of actual experience for what is not generally considered the substance of experience at all.[3] In this the style of the *Commedia* shows affinities with certain kinds of visionary writing, chiefly biblical prophecy, more than with naturalistic or realistic fiction and its meticulous, consciously understated notice of the surfaces of everyday life.

Dante's is, in fact, a style that frequently moves into hyperbole, as distinguished from mere overstatement, in the way it employs hard detail and sometimes an almost mathematical precision in its presentation of the fantastic and grotesque:

> La faccia sua mi parea lunga e grossa
>   come la pina di San Pietro a Roma,
>   e a sua proporzione eran l'altre ossa;
> sì che la ripa, ch'era perizoma
>   dal mezzo in giù, ne mostrava ben tanto
>   di sovra, che di giugnere a la chioma
> tre Frison s'averien dato mal vanto;
>   però ch'i' ne vedea trenta gran palmi
>   dal loco in giù dov' omo affibbia 'l manto.
>
>   (*Inf.* 31.58–66)

His face seemed to me as long and huge as the pine cone of St. Peter's at Rome, and his other bones were in proportion with it; so that the bank, which was an apron to him from his middle downward showed us fully so much of him above, that three Frieslanders would have made ill vaunt to have reached to his hair; for I saw thirty great spans of him down from the place where a man buckles his cloak.

This is Dante's description of one of the fallen giants who surround the last circle of Hell, and it is remarkable for its almost finicky specification of size. A style employing simple overstatement would merely assert hugeness, as Vergil repeatedly calls the people, creatures, and events of the second *Aeneid*, Laocoön's snakes, for instance, *ingens* or *immanis*. But it is one of the hallmarks of Dante's method of description (and perhaps of all true hyperbole, which becomes in its specificity a form of metaphor, as opposed to simple exaggeration, which does not) that it specifies, often very precisely, what seems unspecifiable. Its analogue lies neither in ancient epic nor in modern novel, but in visionary passages of the Bible like John's description of the Heavenly City:

> And he who talked to me had a measuring rod of gold to measure the city and its gates and walls. The city lies four-square, its length the same as its breadth; and he measured the city with his rod, twelve thousand stadia; its length and breadth and height are equal. He also measured its wall, a hundred and forty-four cubits by a man's measure, that is, an angel's. The wall was built of jasper, while the city was pure gold, clear as glass. (Rev. 21:15–18)[4]

We are located squarely in the invisible in a passage such as this, asked to abandon earthly ways of judging and adopt the standards of the absolute, so that man's measure gives way to the angel's and what would appear a contradiction or an impossibility on

earth is simply asserted as a fact of the Heavenly Kingdom—
"pure gold, clear as glass."

But this is to point out Dante's idiosyncracy, his discontinuity
with the ancient tradition to which he otherwise seems so determined to attach his poem. The high medieval character of the
Commedia is undeniable, and yet its affinities with the classical
vision of Vergil are genuine. As we shall see, Dante's conception
of Vergil implies a rejection of the popular medieval version of
the figure, a rejection that further suggests what Dante has profoundly in common with Vergil, a fundamental concern for history and the historical.[5] History is at the heart of Dante's thinking
and vision, in fact at the very heart of his life, and not only the
life he vouchsafes to tell us in the lines of the *Commedia* but also
the life we can glean from other sources as well.[6] Consider only
the best known facts about his career: a talented and learned
public official who put all his energies into the commune of
Florence was rewarded with exile on a trumped-up charge (he
was accused of malfeasance in office), the enduring humiliation
of being beholden for his daily bread, and the official slander of
his reputation which the ruling Neri faction never wearied of
producing. The temptation to shrug his shoulders and fall silent
must have been immense. But instead of withdrawing from public
life, he reentered it in the only way still available to him—in
writing, and not only the *Commedia*, but a host of treatises on
philosophy and language and politics, and a series of epistles to
politicians, prelates, monarchs, and commoners arguing passion-
ately the cause of empire. This is calculated to remind us of
Vergil's Aeneas (Dante himself seems to have made just this
connection), for Dante's refusal to turn his back on his temporal
destiny is the counterpart and complement of the hard lessons
Aeneas must learn that self-sacrifice must be privileged above
self-indulgence, that the public future must always win out over
private memory. Nostalgia, the wish for escape and easy sim-

plification, is peculiarly and especially the poet's problem. One of the reasons the *Aeneid* contains historical prophecies, forward allusions to Augustus, names names, places, and events that have real historical status, is that Vergil must constantly resist the poet's tendency to escape into fantasy or mere wishful thinking.[7] The point of the topical allusions is not flattery of the emperor; they are part of an attempt to keep poetry focused on the world against the imagination's desire for nostalgic abandon. We may imagine Vergil's situation as analogous to his hero's and to Dante's historical predicament in addition. For Aeneas's effort is a constant struggle to keep moving, a struggle against the blandishments of love and fond memory and ease, and his task is simply to get to Italy, where he is to set in motion those events that will later be called Roman history. The desire to escape history, to refuse an authentic temporal destiny, can be found at every level of the *Aeneid* and throughout Dante's *Commedia*.

But another genuine affinity links Dante with the ancient tradition as a whole. The idea of purgation is clearly at the heart of the process in which Dante the pilgrim passes from the Dark Wood, the *selva oscura* in which the poem begins, to the Ancient Wood, the *selva antica* of *Purgatorio* 28.23, in which Vergil returns to his place in Limbo. In his idea of purgation Dante is at one with the ancients on the problem of instinct, the fact that we are given at birth or before, drives, longings, desires, and needs. In this Dante and the ancients could agree, we have no choice—these things are simply given, they are part of our nature. The problem of choice appears when we begin to decide what to do about them, for we can either deny our animal nature and flee from it, we can adopt a polite fiction that it does not exist, or we can approach it creatively and try to incorporate it and use it toward higher ends. The first alternative appears sporadically in the Western tradition, in certain aspects of neo-Platonism, for instance, which preach a simple *voiding* of appetites and desires, a forcible denial of their existence, but it is the second, the creative incorporation of desire, that seems to me to inform the tradition I am trying to describe. For the mainstream of Western thought, classical or Christian, has always associated true civilization, true cultivation of the self not with the voiding of instinct, but with its redirection. And it is this attitude toward the instinctual life with its accompanying corollary that to deny or banish instinct is to invite its recrudescence in even more destructive form that links Dante not only with the Greek poets, whose work in the main he never read, but also with the future that he helped to create. For redirection of instinct toward more productive goals is no less a part of Freud's theory of the unconscious than it is a guiding principle of the majestic resolution of Aeschylus's *Oresteia*, where the Furies, those archaic goddesses of unreflective rage and revenge, are not driven from Athens to dwell in outer darkness (from where—the implication is clear—they might continue to prey upon humanity), but rather given a place in the very center of the city's ritual life.[8] Erinys become Eumenides and make life fertile; Aeneas's *amor* must develop into *pietas*, a respect for ends beyond the immediate pleasure of self-gratification; love of partial goods in Dante's world can and must be redirected toward God who is the source of love and things loved; and finally, according to Freudian theory, our darkest and potentially most destructive wishes are also and necessarily the source of the best of which we are capable; they are what enable the deeply troubled Leonardo to paint the tranquilly contemplative Mona Lisa.

We should very much hesitate to argue that there is anything Freudian about Dante, and in any case such an argument would take us far away from his poetry into areas of his inner life about which we can know nothing. We might, however, speculate that there is something Dantesque about Freud, as well as something Aeschylean and Vergilian. What the psychiatrist shares with the Athenian dramatist and the Roman and Florentine poets is a conviction that the self and the world that it inhabits have an intelligible structure that unify and order them, that in the highest thing or idea that we can conceive, call it God or health or civilization, we can see traces of the lowest, and, conversely, in the lowest thing, no matter how deformed or reduced, we can see the way out and up. For nothing is, or need be, wasted, existing as it does in a relation of meaning to everything else. All these thinkers and poets teach in one way or another that through struggle and suffering and reflection, by submitting the self either individually or collectively to the worst as well as the best that lies buried within it, it is possible to effect a passage from a state of barbarity and disorder to a state of integration and harmony. The passage between these two states is precisely what we call education, a "leading forth" of the self to the best of which it is capable. And any education worthy of the name cannot be a disengaged guided tour, but must rather be a journey in search of spoil, in search of the energy necessary to complete the desired transformation. Call it education, call it cure, call it, with Dante, purgation, it can never be simply a voiding of the self, but must always be a rechanneling, a reorganization in the hope of higher integration. It is interesting to recall in this context that Freud chose as the epigraph for *The Interpretation of Dreams* a line from Vergil: "Flectere si nequeo superos Acheronta movebo" ("If I can sway / No heavenly hearts I'll rouse the world below" [7.312; 425–26]).[9] The tapping of infernal energy to accomplish work in the daylight is as old as ancient epic and as new as modern psychology.

2 VERGIL'S MISSING NAME

It so happens that the *Oresteia* of Aeschylus offers an entry to the *Commedia* from a different, if closely related, direction. At the end of *The Eumenides* the Furies are not only incorporated, they are renamed, the Erinys become Eumenides and settle down to Athenian life. The renaming does not apparently signify any change in their nature, for Aeschylus makes it clear that they are the same rather physically unlovely creatures they have always been. What the renaming does signify, one might argue, is a change in us, in our relation to the Furies, in our way of understanding them and thus of dealing with them. This power of names to change understanding may seem a kind of primitive magic and finally an empty ritual gesture. But it is far more than that, for Aeschylus knew that names and words—whole languages, in fact—define the world for us, establish us in our relation to it. To change the name of the Furies from Erinys, which probably means something like "bringers of discord,"[10] to Eumenides, which means the gracious, well-disposed goddesses, is to effect a change in our relation to them. To be properly magical the renaming would have to cause a change in the Furies' nature or substance: Aeschylus is clear that this is not the case. We know that the foreign enemies of Athens have but to attack and they will discover that for *them* the Furies will always be Erinys, bringers of discord. The change in name effects a change in relation and understanding. There is nothing magical about it: the Furies now protect the *polis* they formerly threatened to destroy. Their energy has been redirected outward.

It is with these problems of language and naming in mind that we come to consider the rather mysterious appearance of Vergil in the first canto of the *Commedia*. The scene is one of the best known in the poem: the pilgrim has tried to climb a hill, but he has been stopped by three strange and rather clearly allegorical beasts, and particularly by a she-wolf, the third in this trio. Vergil appears and, apparently unaware of any emergency, proceeds to introduce himself in what must strike us in the circumstances as a rather leisurely and roundabout way (*Inf.* 1.67–75). He does not name himself at all, but rather recites his parentage, the place and time of his birth; he furnishes the scene of his earthly activity and then tells what that activity consisted in:

> Poeta fui, e cantai di quel giusto
> figliuol d'Anchise che venne di Troia,
> poi che 'l superbo Iliön fu combusto.
>
> (73–75)

I was a poet, and I sang of that just son of Anchises who came from Troy after proud Ilium was burned.

This is odd. Why does not Vergil just say his name and be done with it? Dante, who, Vergil later intimates, knows the *Aeneid* by heart, must surely have also known these rather sketchy biographical details with which Vergil here laboriously identifies himself. But the suppression of the proper name is in fact deliberate and is furthermore closely related to an essential stylistic feature of the *Commedia* we will deal with later. For the moment we will assume that this roundabout introduction is something more than a piece of quaint medieval diction and that Vergil is here, as always, trying to teach the pilgrim something.

Let us briefly recall some aspects of the medieval popular tradition surrounding Vergil. It is well known that Vergil was the subject of a rather startling body of fiction in the Middle Ages, that the collective imagination of Late Antiquity and the Dark Ages made of him, through a series of popular stories and poems, a kind of wondrous magician able to perform amazing feats of technology, to build bridges across oceans, to protect cities from attack by ingenious early warning devices. The medieval Vergil of the popular accounts could fly, make himself invisible, suspend natural law, and foretell the future.[11] The text of the *Aeneid* became a sort of medieval *I Ching*, and in performing the *sortes vergilianae* people told fortunes by applying to their own lives randomly selected verses from the poem. Such stories and beliefs are perhaps harmless enough, yet they also suggest certain perennial tendencies of the human mind with which Dante was very much concerned and which he may have considered dangerous, insofar as they promised what they could not possibly deliver, held out a false promise to the reader that he could escape his humanity or avoid the burden of his earthly destiny. For the fictional world which the medieval stories of Vergil's supposed exploits project is precisely magical, a world where problems can be solved without difficulty, where the present can be controlled and the future avoided because it can be so easily predicted by the mere opening of a book. In this world the figure of Vergil himself is treated in an oddly and cavalierly antihistorical way: he seems to be everywhere at any time, for his biographers, if they can be called that, have him appear all around the Mediterranean, wherever people need him, to meet situations that apparently occurred long after his historical demise in 19 B.C. Even when the writer is too sophisticated to assert that Vergil was present after his death, his real effects are still felt through some wondrous invention he has left behind or through some miracle attributed to the magical efficacy of his bones or tomb.

Related to these productions of sheer fantasy are the somewhat more serious, or at least more seriously undertaken, attempts to find in Vergil's writing prophecies of the birth of Christ, the fourth *Eclogue* being the obvious point of departure. In these works, although the writers do not assert Vergil's actual presence in the Middle Ages, the poet is nevertheless implicitly seen as escaping time and history through his prophetic gifts, as avoiding the very fate that Dante's conception of Vergil's character seems to resubject him to, the tragic fate of having been born too soon, of missing through an accident of history the New Dispensation in the form of a saving belief in Christ. That Dante suggests that Vergil did in fact do something like predict the birth of Christ in his fourth *Eclogue* is clear from what Statius has to say in *Purgatorio* 22:

> "Tu prima m'invïasti
> verso Parnaso a ber ne le sue grotte,
> e prima appresso Dio m'alluminasti.
> Facesti come quei che va di notte,
> che porta il lume dietro e sé non giova,
> ma dopo sé fa le persone dotte,
> quando dicesti: 'Secol si rinova;
> torna giustizia e primo tempo umano,
> e progenïe scende da ciel nova.'
> Per te poeta fui, per te cristiano."
>
> (64–73)

"You it was who first sent me toward Parnassus to drink in its caves, and you who first did light me on to God. You were like one who goes by night and carries the light behind him and profits not himself, but makes those wise who follow him, when you said, 'The ages are renewed; Justice returns and the first age of man, and a new progeny descends from heaven.' Through you I was a poet, through you a Christian."

But notice that Statius is careful to say that Vergil himself did not understand the import of what he was saying.[12] He said in his poetry more than he knew, just as Statius, who was a convert but did not proclaim his conversion in poetry, said less than he knew. It is but one of many times when we are made to feel the pathos of Vergil's situation, to understand what better use he would have made of the New Dispensation than many of those who in fact possess it through an apparent accident of birth. Statius's admitted lack of courage only serves to make Vergil seem the more quietly heroic, the more selfless, one who has sacrificed himself for others, in fact the embodiment of that *pietas* his own poem continually praises. He has remained at least consistent with the principles set forth in his poetry, where Statius has clearly not remained consistent with the principles set forth in his. Yet this is the position to which Dante adheres, for to make Vergil a magician or vulgar prophet able to avoid the future would be precisely to deprive him of the dignity of his historical destiny (the sort of dignity that his own poem also continually praises), of his investment of himself in history, an investment with which one enters on the road to salvation, although one still may, like Vergil, fall by the way, but without which one cannot even begin the journey. It is always a temptation for the mind to try to escape history, and it is precisely this temptation that Dante and the figure of Vergil in the *Commedia* rigorously refuse.

This then is the meaning, or one of the meanings, of Vergil's odd way of introducing himself in *Inferno* 1: he insists on his status not as a fantastic magician, as a practitioner of the impossible, but as a historical being; he reinserts himself into the stream of earthly life and event from which the popular legends had removed him, refuses the image of an immortal fictional character which Late Antiquity and the Middle Ages had conferred upon him. His simple name, the proper name by which a whole tradition has come to know him—Vergil—has become contaminated by the popularizers, and so Vergil himself refuses to use it, retreats back into an account of the simple historical facts of his being, strips himself of the burden of false assumption with which a minor literary genre of the Middle Ages had invested him. "No, not a living man," he says on first appearing to the pilgrim, "though once I was" (*Inf.* 1.67), as if to insist that he has enjoyed no special, privileged, magical mode of being on earth, but is a man born of men who lived and died and has remained dead. And this too is an instance of that *pietas* that Dante's Vergil so consistently displays, for, as we are reminded repeatedly throughout the first two canticles of the poem, Vergil's only hope of immortality is his fame on earth, his survival in human memory: to refuse the false prestige of a debased tradition, which, no matter how naively distorting of one's real historical being, is nevertheless a way of keeping one's name alive, is to value true honor and one's genuine usefulness to those who come after over false honor, the merely self-serving preservation of one's name by any means. It is, as we shall see, to make a future possible.

This rejection of the medieval Vergil in order to restore the historical Vergil is perhaps the first, but certainly not the last, occasion in the poem where we can watch Dante the poet enclosing and incorporating other kinds of fictions in order to turn them to his own ends. The effect is often rather eerie: it is as if characters who properly belong in different *kinds* of stories, characters from romance or ancient heroic epic or popular farce, had wandered into an alien order of being and were now being scrutinized according to its more rigorous standards. We speak of Dante's style sometimes as if it were all of a piece: but consider the enormous number of different *kinds* of utterances, different kinds of styles that his poem offers us, all juxtaposed and thrown together as if to call attention to the mix. There is the heroic bravura of Ulysses (*Inf.* 26), which sounds so odd when it is followed immediately by the contemporary political jargon with which Dante answers Guida da Montefeltro's anguished question about the current state of Romagna; or the heraldic jargon of the usurers ("Let the sovereign knight come who will bring the pouch with the three goats!" [*Inf.* 17.72–73]), which we can become aware of *as* a style merely by laying it alongside the earthy Florentine slang of Brunetto Latini. T. S. Eliot remarked that the effect of Dante's poetry was to make you see what he saw, his similes are there "merely to make you see more clearly how the people looked."[13] It seems reasonable to say that the effect of Dante's poetry is at least equally to make us hear what he heard. To privilege the eye as Eliot does is to render the poetry as naive description, where as a matter of fact it is anything but naive. Dante's poetry is intensely focused on style, on the mode of utterance, and it always asks us to see what a given style means, how it rearranges the world, what burden of assumption lies hidden within it.

But there is something else about this assertion that Dante's is a predominantly visual poetry, for the visual image, the portrait (Eliot's remark about the similes showing us "more clearly how the people looked") leads away from the process of history to the moment of form, the frozen posture, whereas the whole thrust of the *Commedia* seems to be precisely in the opposite direction, as Dante resubmits frozen images to the heat of history, melting them down and recirculating them, testing them against the strain that history puts upon them. We have already seen the figure of Vergil performing a similar operation on his own frozen, fictionalized image, his reinsertion of himself into historical time and process. He appears to the pilgrim in the Dark Wood not merely to strip himself of an antihistorical tradition, but also to lead the pilgrim, that confused, wandering, endangered spiritual exile, back to history as well, to reconcile him to his historical calling in the world, to fit him with his authentic temporal destiny which, as we will later learn from Cacciaguida in *Paradiso*, is precisely to write the *Commedia*. Here again, we will be better off to forget portraits and attend to language, to utterance, for Dante's language is an instrument far more than it is a mirror, a passive receptacle of experience; it is a highly active phenomenon, fully transitive toward the experience it embodies. It is not content to draw pictures; it performs operations.

Beatrice's injunction to Vergil in the scene in the second canto of *Inferno* where she descends into Hell to send the poet to the bewildered pilgrim is worthy of attention in this respect:

'Or movi, e con la tua parola ornata
e con ciò c'ha mestieri al suo campare,
l'aiuta sì ch'i' ne sia consolata.'

(67–69)

"Go now, and with your fair speech and with whatever is needful
for his deliverance, assist him so that it may console me."

This may mean simply, "Try to talk him out of the difficulty he
is having," but it means more as well. It also means something
like "lend him your tongue," give the aid that only an earlier
poet can give a later, an earlier poet who has already worked out
a diction capable of making profound (if ultimately incomplete)
sense of the universe. Thus, what Beatrice means by Vergil's *parola
ornata*, his "fair speech," is partly the text of the *Aeneid* itself.

Vergil's introduction of himself in *Inferno* 1 also has some
bearing on this question. He tells the pilgrim,

"Poeta fui, e cantai di quel giusto
figliuol d'Anchise che venne di Troia,
poi che 'l superbo Ilïón fu combusto.
Ma tu perché ritorni a tanta noia?
perché non sali il dilettoso monte
ch'è principio e cagion di tutta gioia?"

(73–78)

"I was a poet, and I sang of that just son of Anchises who came
from Troy after proud Ilium was burned. But you, why do you
return to so much woe? Why do you not climb the delectable
mountain, the source and cause of every happiness?"

The abrupt shift in reference indicated by the "But you" creates
a discontinuity that actually alerts us to a continuity at a deeper
level, for the rhyme words here in Italian drive the point home:
Troia, noia, gioia—Troy, woe, happiness, as if the journey of
Aeneas were a paradigm of the journey from woe to happiness,

as if the sadness at the Fall of Troy and the suffering of Aeneas were somehow the pilgrim's sadness and suffering too. "I am not Aeneas," the pilgrim will protest in the next canto (32), as he is losing his nerve and having second thoughts about the arduous journey Vergil has proposed. But ironically he becomes in that moment of utterance a version of the uneducated Aeneas, who also at first shrinks from the burden imposed upon him and would remain in the smoldering ruins of Troy rather than risk himself on the unknown sea and submit to his high historical calling.[14]

The interlocking form of *terza rima* proves its value at the very outset of the poem, for not only does it absorb the action of the *Aeneid* and the poet who wrote it, but having absorbed them, can allow them to turn and in their turn absorb the character of the confused pilgrim within the poem, reinstall him in the ordered vision of history that the *Aeneid* provides by establishing him in parallel relation with its hero. We have here a purified or corrected version of the *sortes vergilianae*: instead of the text of the *Aeneid* being fragmented and reduced to fit the life of a single person, the life of a single person is expanded to fit the text, and in the process no false promises of avoiding the suffering of the future are offered, although a meaning, a direction is conferred upon that suffering. The passage is an instance of the way Vergil, precisely with his "fair speech," can lead the pilgrim back to history. It is also a foreshadowing, in the way it transports Vergil and the action of his poem into the flow of Italian *terza rima*, of the way in which Dante will save Vergil for history, keep him afloat in the tide of historical change.

But it may still seem paradoxical to assert that Vergil comes to lead the pilgrim back to history when in fact he immediately takes him to the otherworld, the place of and for eternity, a place outside of time and process. Does not the inscription over Hellgate assert precisely a distance from human history, a coming into being before the inauguration of historical time and continuing existence after historical time has been brought to an end in the Last Judgment?

DINANZI A ME NON FUOR COSE CREATE

SE NON ETTERNE, E IO ETTERNO DURO.

(*Inf.* 3.7–8)

BEFORE ME NOTHING WAS CREATED

IF NOT ETERNAL, AND ETERNAL I ENDURE.

But this is, of course, the container speaking and not the things it contains. The *souls* that the pilgrim meets, and not only those in Hell but those in Purgatory and Paradise as well, are never presented to us simply as a series of examples of sin or saintliness, mere points in an abstract moral schema, but rather as the results of a process, the artifacts of the various ways in which they have lived their lives in time. In the results that we meet we can always see the traces of the process by which this result came to be, and it is this sense of historical depth, the sense that things do not simply exist but came to be this way, that gives Dante's poetry its excitement, its concreteness, its unfailing ability to give us the feeling of real presence. And here again it is often the availability of Vergil's fair speech that helps Dante to recover this historical dimension.

Let us consider a well-known passage: the pilgrim and Vergil have entered the second circle of Hell, the abode of the lustful, and the pilgrim quite naturally asks his guide who these people are. Vergil's reply is as always worthy of scrutiny:

"La prima di color di cui novelle

tu vuo' saper," mi disse quelli allotta,

"fu imperadrice di molte favelle.

A vizio di lussuria fu sì rotta,

che libito fé licito in sua legge,

per tòrre il biasmo in che era condotta.

Ell' è Semiramìs, di cui si legge
  che succedette a Nino e fu sua sposa:
  tenne la terra che 'l Soldan corregge.
L'altra è colei che s'ancise amorosa,
  e ruppe fede al cener di Sicheo;
  poi è Cleopatràs lussurïosa."

(5.52–63)

"The first of these of whom you wish to know," he said to me
then, "was empress of many tongues. She was so given to lechery
that she made lust licit in her law, to take away the blame she
had incurred. She is Semiramis, of whom we read that she succeeded
Ninus and had been his wife: she held the land the Sultan rules.
The next is she who slew herself for love and broke faith to the
ashes of Sichaeus; next is wanton Cleopatra."

Semiramis gives us no trouble because Vergil, after a long description of what is really important about her—her moral history—finally deigns to name her; the same is true of Cleopatra,
who gets a kind of minimum of attention in the short qualifier
lussurïosa. But notice that Dido, of all people, a character in
Vergil's own poem, gets short shrift as "she that slew herself for
love and broke faith to the ashes of Sichaeus." The effect is almost
brutal but makes a powerful point. What Vergil appears to be
trying to teach the pilgrim is that any prestige that has attached
itself to the name of Dido, either because she is a prominent and
colorful character in a famous Latin epic, or because she had
become a sympathetic heroine in a whole series of medieval ro-
mances, must now be stripped away; we must understand finally
the moral content of her career, of her personal history, not the
glitter of her image.

The necessity of such an understanding is underscored by the
bearing of Francesca herself, who is named only by the pilgrim
in a moment of morally culpable sympathy with her (5.116),

never by Dante the poet, nor by Vergil. For what is the whole tendency of Francesca's speech but an attempt to insert herself into a romance, to become the heroine of the kind of story in which adultery is a glamorous norm and the conventional postures of swooning passion the goal and end of life itself? And in some sense she succeeds in this: her identification with Guinevere in the Lancelot romance is total, so complete we might say that she in her turn never names Guinevere, not because she wants to retreat from the prestige of the name, but because she has in her own mind merged so completely with the fictional character that she feels no more need to name the character than she does to name herself.[15] She and Paolo have proceeded to act out the romance they have begun by merely reading, from reading a book they have, as it were, lapsed into allowing a book to write them, and they have thus abandoned their lives in history to a common death in fantasy. "Several times," says Francesca, "that reading urged our eyes to meet and took the color from our faces" ("Per più fïate li occhi ci sospinse / quella lettura, e scolorocci il viso" [130–31]), a passage in which the language dramatizes for us the very process of becoming a fiction, of dying into text. The verb *scolorare* means the same thing (in Dante's Italian) as *discolorare*, which means not only "to change color," but also "to lose color" (compare Vergil's use of *discolor* in the *Aeneid* to describe the eerie gleam of the golden bough [6.204], and Dante's own use of *discolorare* to describe the withering of grass [*Purg.* 11.116]). It is as if Paolo and Francesca were fading out of life in the very process of reading.

The effect is rather like the curiously impersonal one two lines further on (133), where Francesca describes Guinevere's smile as "il disïato riso" ("the longed-for smile"), which is to say the conventional and mandatory event in the courtly romance. The impersonal construction with the passive participle performs an important operation on this action of Guinevere's: we must ask *who* smiled, because Francesca's mode of speech has not only turned the action of smiling into a static ornament, the smile, but has suppressed the face on which that ornament has appeared. She has plucked the event from history, the field of moral choice, or rather prevented it from emerging from the fiction in which it began; an action has become a thing, in which form it no longer solicits the crucial moral questions we should be asking of it. It is in this sense that we can say that Francesca's very language reenacts the process by which she came to be where we now find her.[16]

Nor is this all: what we have been examining is Francesca's earthly career as we can reconstruct it from her speech. But we notice that she is still at it, still trying to enter the prestigious world of romance and love literature as she understands it. This is the meaning of the fact that in her answer to the pilgrim she speaks like a character in the *Aeneid*:

> E quella a me: "Nessun maggior dolore
>   che ricordarsi del tempo felice
>   ne la miseria; e ciò sa 'l tuo dottore.
> Ma s'a conoscer la prima radice
>   del nostro amor tu hai cotanto affetto,
>   dirò come colui che piange e dice."
>
> (121–26)

And she to me, "There is no greater sorrow than to recall, in wretchedness, the happy time; and this your teacher knows. But if you have such great desire to know the first root of our love, I will tell as one who weeps and tells."

Vergil certainly ought to know what Francesca is talking about, for he wrote the lines that inspire the lines she speaks. They are, of course, famous, a set-piece in their own right:

'infandum, regina, iubes renovare dolorem.

.   .   .   .

sed si tantus amor casus cognoscere nostros
et breviter Troiae supremum audire laborem,
quamquam animus meminisse horret luctuque refugit,
incipiam.'   (2.3, 10–13)

"Sorrow too deep to tell, your majesty,
You order me to tell and feel once more.

.   .   .   .

But if so great desire
Moves you to hear the tale of our disasters,
Briefly recalled, the final throes of Troy,
However I may shudder at the memory
And shrink again in grief, let me begin."
(1–2, 13–17)

There is profound irony here, for Francesca cannot merely
borrow the impressive roll of Vergil's majestic periodic sentence,
she must, in spite of herself, borrow its meaning as well. The
lines in the *Aeneid* are, of course, spoken by Aeneas to Dido, and
it seems as if Francesca with some part of her mind were trying
to take by force what has been given freely to the pilgrim in the
second canto, trying in fact to enforce a parallel between herself
and Aeneas when one can no longer exist. We know that she is
not at all like Aeneas (she is indeed far more like Dido, with
whom she shares the second circle), because she has retreated
permanently from history into passion, whereas Aeneas, after a
similar but temporary lapse, reassumes his historical destiny. The
pilgrim's words in the second canto—"I am not Aeneas" (32)—
words that express a fear that he immediately conquers, would
come curiously true in the mouth of Francesca. Indeed, she is *not*
Aeneas.

Francesca not only tells a story, she establishes a pattern as well. She is but the first of a whole series of souls whom the pilgrim and Vergil will meet who have staked their immortality on words or books or fictions, and in so doing have made the tragic discovery that they have entered a closed world from which there is no hope of release. We might consider in this context Dante's old and respected teacher Brunetto Latini (*Inf.* 15), a prestigious figure in his own right in his days in Florence, who is now spending eternity with his fellow sodomites. His parting words to the pilgrim are, "Let my *Treasure*, in which I yet live, be commended to you, and I ask no more" ("Sieti raccomandato il mio Tesoro, / nel qual io vivo ancora, e più non cheggio" [15.119–20]). Brunetto's best-known book now constitutes his only claim to continuing prestige, to fame, to the preservation of his memory in the minds of men. As with Francesca, the flight into books includes a retreat from history, for in choosing the sterility of homosexuality, Brunetto has refused procreation, or, more exactly, has chosen the lesser procreation of authorship, chosen to create books rather than offspring and has thus betrayed that aspect of love or desire that makes human continuity possible, that gives history, so to speak, the human material to continue. It would seem that the sterility of Francesca's adulterous passion and the far more understated sterility of Brunetto's homosexuality are closely related.

There is more here too: again, as with Francesca, much of the tragic irony in the situation is precipitated by an allusion to the *Aeneid*. This time it is the pilgrim who "speaks Vergil":

> "Se fosse tutto pieno il mio dimando,"
> rispuos' io lui, "voi non sareste ancora
> de l'umana natura posto in bando;
> ché'n la mente m'è fitta, e or m'accora,
> la cara e buona imagine paterna

di voi quando nel mondo ad ora ad ora
m'insegnavate come l'uom s'etterna."

(15.79–85)

"If my prayer were all fulfilled," I answered him, "you would not
yet be banished from human nature, for in my memory is fixed,
and now saddens my heart, the dear, kind, paternal image of you,
when in the world hour by hour you taught me how man makes
himself eternal."

The canto is shot through with Vergilian echoes, so that sometimes Dante's language seems to become a sort of pastiche, but
this particular scene and situation as well as the words are calculated to make us think of another meeting of a father and son
in the underworld, the meeting of Aeneas and Anchises. Particularly the phrase "la cara e buona imagine paterna" ("the dear,
kind, paternal image of you") can be usefully compared to
Aeneas's words on meeting his father:

'tua me, genitor, tua tristis imago
saepius occurrens haec limina tendere adegit.'

(6.695–96)

"Your ghost,
Your sad ghost, father, often before my mind,
Impelled me to the threshold of this place."

(932–34)

The crucial word here is *imago*, that is, "image," Dante's word
imagine. But the pilgrim calls Brunetto's image stored up in his
memory "paternal," *paterna*, from Latin *pater*, whereas in the
corresponding passage of the *Aeneid* Vergil does not use the word
pater at all, but rather the far more specific *genitor*, which means
"sire," a biological father, our word "progenitor," one who has
begotten. The implication is clear: Brunetto is and can be a father

to the pilgrim only in a very limited, a very partial sense. He has taught the young Dante how one "makes himself immortal" through writing, through poetry, through fame, but what he has left in silence the *Aeneid* supplies by offering us an image of a true father and son at a cardinal point in history, at the moment before a future, that precisely which Brunetto can never have, is unfolded in the grand prophecy of Roman greatness with which the sixth *Aeneid* concludes. It is interesting to note that when the pilgrim does meet a real father, a real progenitor, his great-great grandfather Cacciaguida in Paradise, the scene includes not only backward glances to the canto of Brunetto Latini, but allusions to this same scene in the *Aeneid* that we have been considering.[17] Again and again Cacciaguida is compared to a jewel, to a gem, until finally Dante calls him his "treasure," the title of Brunetto's book deprived of its capital letter ("La luce in che rideva il mio tesoro" [*Par.* 17. 121]). And when he first meets Cacciaguida in *Paradiso* 15, the passage from the *Aeneid* comes spontaneously forward:

> né si partì la gemma dal suo nastro,
>   ma per la lista radïal trascorse,
>   che parve foco dietro ad alabastro.
> Sì pïa l'ombra d'Anchise si porse,
>   se fede merta nostra maggior musa,
>   quando in Eliso del figlio s'accorse.
>   (*Par.* 15.22–27)

nor did the gem depart from its ribbon, but coursed along the radial strip, and seemed like fire behind alabaster. With like affection did the shade of Anchises stretch forward (if our greatest Muse merits belief), when in Elysium he perceived his son.

But there is something more yet in the meeting with Brunetto that we must examine. Dante begins the canto with a curious word for the stone embankment on which the pilgrim and Vergil are walking to avoid the burning sand. He says (*Inf.* 15.1), "Now one of the hard margins bears us on" ("Ora cen porta l'un de' duri margini"). The word *margini* is oddly redistributed in the words of the succeeding lines, in *argini* with which it rhymes, in *imagine* (10), in *maraviglia* (24). One has the sense that it refers to the embankment but suggests the margin of a text or page, especially since it is located so close to the marginal pause between cantos. And indeed we do have the sense later on, when Brunetto has appeared, of looking into a text or story that one cannot enter bodily, a sense that is strengthened by the Vergilian allusion in lines 17–19: "and each looked at us as men look at one another under a new moon at dusk" ("e ciascuna / ci riguardava come suol da sera / guardare uno altro sotto nuova luna"). The allusion might well be to Aeneas's first glimpse of Dido in the underworld:

> Phoenissa recens a vulnere Dido
> errabat silva in magna; quam Troius heros
> ut primum iuxta stetit agnovitque per umbras
> obscuram, qualem primo qui surgere mense
> aut videt aut vidisse putat per nubila lunam.
>
> (6.450–54)

> with her fatal wound still fresh,
> Phoenician Dido wandered the deep wood.
> The Trojan captain paused nearby and knew
> Her dim form in the dark, as one who sees,
> Early in the month, or thinks to have seen, the moon
> Rising through cloud, all dim.   (606–11)

The unreality of the scene, its remoteness from Aeneas (pathetically remote: Dido has been so present to him in Carthage) is stressed here in the epanorthotic phrase "aut videt aut vidisse putat" ("who sees . . . or thinks to have seen"). The *lugentes campi*, the "mourning fields," have the status of fiction for Aeneas, the bearer of history who is not allowed the luxury of mourning.

This is perhaps why Vergil fills them with names from myth and story, Phaedra, Eriphyle, Evadne, Pasiphae (445–47); and this is part of the reason Dido turns from Aeneas without a word: she exists now in a wholly different order of being.

Dante has reworked the Vergilian scene boldly. Here is no shadowy necessity, no mysterious principle at work that forbids people to touch and causes them to turn away in tragic silence. Brunetto is, rather, garrulous, and he speaks his own authentic Florentine idiom, naming himself proudly even after the pilgrim has recognized him and called him by name (lines 30 and 32). Moreover, Brunetto touches the hem of the pilgrim's garment ("che mi prese / per lo lembo" [23–24]), an action that would be out of place in Vergil's shadow-world of figures who dissolve in the grasp of the living. Brunetto is in every sense a presence in this scene, but his presence finally serves only to emphasize his remoteness for the pilgrim, the man who, like Aeneas, must move on, must not linger with those who have forever stopped. For here is Vergil, curiously silent, a true father and teacher, presiding over the meeting, pausing while Dante bids a tender farewell to a failed and incomplete father and teacher. The way in which the pilgrim identifies Vergil for Brunetto is significant. "Who is this that shows the way?" Brunetto asks, and the pilgrim replies:

> "Là sù di sopra, in la vita serena,"
>> rispuos' io lui, "mi smarri' in una valle,
>> avanti che l'età mia fosse piena.
> Pur ier mattina le volsi le spalle:
>> questi m'apparve, tornand' io in quella,
>> e reducemi a ca per questo calle."
>
> *(Inf.* 15.49–54)

"There above, in the bright life," I answered him, "I went astray in a valley, before my age was at the full. Only yesterday morning

I turned my back on it. He appeared to me, as I was returning into it, and by this path he leads me home."

The lines recapitulate an action with which Brunetto can have nothing to do. The reply, which must be as dark to Brunetto as Brunetto's later prophecy is to the pilgrim, uses a set of symbols with which we are familiar, because we have read the first canto of the poem, but which must be mysterious to Brunetto. There is, of course, reason for this: the pilgrim is being polite to Brunetto, being careful to lay no claim to the prestige inherent in the fact that he is in the company of Vergil instead of the company of a somewhat less well known poet of Dante's Florence. The modern reader is if anything more sensitive to the disparity between Vergil, whose name needs no explanation, and Brunetto Latini, whose name may send him in search of a footnote.

But there is more here, for the passage works oddly with its time references, in the way it moves from "before my age was at the full" to "Only yesterday morning." "Before my age was at the full" must surely refer to Dante's age at the time he went astray in what he here calls "a valley," that is, the Dark Wood of the first canto, where he was "Midway in the journey of our life," which is, of course, a matter of thirty-five years, half the biblical three score and ten. The passage effects an abrupt shift (more abrupt in Italian, for the two time references are in adjacent lines) from the relatively leisurely time of Dante's career in Florence (the thirty-five years before he went astray in the Dark Wood), the career with which Brunetto has had to do and to which he refers immediately after this passage (55–60), to the compressed, fuller time of the journey through the otherworld ("Only yesterday morning"), in which Dante has already learned so much more of so much more consequence than in all his thirty-five years in life. There could be no politer, gentler way of telling Brunetto, as the pilgrim surely does so obliquely here, that he must make haste, that he cannot linger, that there is still much to be seen and so little time to see it in the company of the new master. There can finally be no comparison between the education under Vergil, a vastly expanded lesson in "how man makes himself eternal," and the education under Brunetto whose recollection of his own tutelage becomes in this light pathetic in a way he does not perhaps understand.

We remember in this context Brunetto's touching of the hem of the pilgrim's garment, that gesture which only seems to establish a real continuity between the two men, for we now realize that it goes only as far as the hem, *il lembo* (compare *limbo*, the "fringe" of Hell), the margin of the pilgrim's being, just as the pilgrim goes no further toward Brunetto than the hard margin of the brook, *la margine dura* on which he stands. Brunetto is at last only a story, a bearer of a text, for so the pilgrim calls Brunetto's dark prophecy of the future:

> "Ciò che narrate di mio corso scrivo,
>   e serbolo a chiosar con altro testo
>   a donna che saprà, s'a lei arrivo."
> (88–90)

"That which you tell me of my course I write, and keep with a text to be glossed by a lady who will know how, if I reach her."

The diction here, the pilgrim's assertion that he will write (*scrivo*) what Brunetto has told him, probably rests on the radical metaphor of the book of memory which we encounter at the beginning of *Inferno* 2: "o mente che scrivesti ciò ch'io vidi" ("O memory that wrote down what I saw").[18] But it also suggests the notion of a text which we have been stressing, for, if the memory is a book, the mind of the pilgrim is a text in the process of being written in the journey through the otherworld. It will be complete when the journey has been finished. Brunetto is already complete, although he is scarcely perfected: he can only form a part of the perfected text that will be both the fully educated pilgrim and the text of the *Commedia* that he will write.

3 THE LANGUAGE OF THE TRIBE

The flight from history, restated in the meeting with Brunetto Latini as a flight from procreation, is a concern that appears at all levels of Dante's poem, informing and giving shape and tying together widely dispersed reaches of the text. And the flight seems always bound up with the problems of language, of fiction, of style, of all those linguistic shelters in which we have seen various figures in Dante's poem taking refuge from the historical winds that blow through it and in part inspire it, give it breath.[19] Many of the damned show a curious inability to distinguish between the metaphorical and the real and a curious tendency to treat symbols, words, signs, specialized jargons as if they had reality in themselves, rather than deriving their value from the fact that they point beyond themselves to meanings.[20]

We meet the extreme case of this disability in the gibberish of the giant Nimrod (*Inf.* 31), in the language that only he possesses, but the extreme is related to a whole spectrum of attempts in Hell to raid the public domain of language and symbol and appropriate it for the self, to force it to work for one's own immortality. Guido da Montefeltro's story (*Inf.* 27) records among other things just such an attempt to subjugate the language of salvation, the symbols of Holy Church, and make it private property. It is thus fitting that Guido's interlocutor should be the infamous simonist Pope Boniface VIII, for simony, the buying and selling of ecclesiastical office, is nothing but an attempt to do much the same thing, to turn what belongs to society and, of course, ultimately to God, into private gain. One idea that seems to run through this whole stretch of the *Commedia* where Guido's story is found is the idea of theft, and not only in the cantos that deal specifically with thieves (24–25), but also in the canto of Ulysses, in his and Diomedes' theft of the Palladium from Troy (26.63); in the flames that move in the ditch and, as Dante says, "not one shows its theft, and each steals away a sinner" (26.41–42); or in Boniface's theft of the keys to Heaven (for so Dante understood Boniface's ascent to the papacy after the suspicious resignation of Celestine V), those keys, which as Boniface cynically remarks, "my predecessor did not hold dear" (27.105); or finally in the little scene at Guido's death where the black cherub accuses St. Francis of trying to cheat him of his prey, of stealing it from him (27.114–20).[21]

We recall that Guido had become a Franciscan in the hope that it would serve to save him. It has not, of course, and a consideration of his way of speaking can help to tell us why. Guido speaks, for instance, of the cord that is part of the Franciscan habit as "quel capestro / che solea fare i suoi cinti più macri" ("that cord which used to make its wearers lean" [27.92–93]), as if the monk's clothes were invested with a magical power for saving the man who wears them, rather than merely being the visible sign of what is in fact a spiritual choice. There is a crucial confusion of exterior and interior here, of matter and spirit, of mental acts and solid things, a confusion that appears also in Boniface's speech concerning the keys of Heaven:

> 'Lo ciel poss' io serrare e diserrare,
> come tu sai; però son due le chiavi
> che 'l mio antecessor non ebbe care.'
>
> (103–5)

'I can lock and unlock Heaven, as you know; for the keys are two, which my predecessor did not hold dear.'

This is to speak of the keys of Heaven as if they had some kind of tangible reality, when in fact if they exist as tangible keys at all, and are not simply the symbolic keys that Christ bestows upon Peter in Matthew's gospel, they are clearly ceremonial in their nature, the outward and visible sign of an invisible, essentially spiritual reality, the inward meaning of ecclesiastical office. To treat them as if their primary reality were physical, a reality one could possess, is precisely to appropriate them, to try to turn them into a form of property, to insist that they exist for one's private ends and uses.

Something of the same sort of intense insistence on an office, a position of public trust, as a private preserve for the self is implicit in Pier della Vigna's remark about his service to Emperor Frederick II:

> "Io son colui che tenni ambo le chiavi
>   del cor di Federigo, e che le volsi,
>   serrando e diserrando, sì soavi,
>   che dal secreto suo quasi ogn' uom tolsi."
>   (*Inf.* 13.58–61)

"I am he who held both the keys of Frederick's heart, and turned them, locking and unlocking, so softly that from his secrets I kept almost every one."

It is the intense privacy of both men, the one the servant of empire, the other the servant of the Church, that is so disturbing. We sense that it is the *quasi*, the "almost," in the phrase "almost every one" that marks the intensity of Pier's frustration: it designates his failure wholly to colonize a public spiritual reality for himself. And the ultimate meaning of Boniface's way of speaking about the keys of Heaven is the same as the ultimate meaning of the way he came by them in the first place: as we have already seen, he stole them. Simony, like all the names Dante uses for specific sins, does not mean *simply* the sale of ecclesiastical offices; it points rather to the whole appropriative tendency that is finally the organizing principle of Boniface's being. Boniface has attempted to seize for himself not only ecclesiastical offices, but the very symbols with which the Church attempts to point beyond itself to the reality of God. His is a fundamental and complete, rather than an incidental and isolated, refusal to understand the ways in which the universe is meaningful.

The same can be said of Guido, who calls the pope's words *argomenti gravi* ("weighty arguments" [27.106]), and makes it seem in context as if the word "weighty" had been emptied of its metaphorical content, that is, of its meaning of "serious," and now contained as a kind of residue only the original physical meaning of "heavy." The pope's arguments are weighty for Guido because they implicitly appeal to his superstitious attraction to the glamour of objects, to the prestige that physical presence has over the harder-to-grasp concerns of the spirit. We are perhaps meant to enjoy the irony of what was, by all accounts, one of the most sophisticated minds of the age reduced to a primitive sort of magical manipulation, rehearsing its logic of things in a vain effort to find where it went wrong. No other technique of exposing the false prestige accorded to wiliness, guile, or "foxiness," to make use of Guido's own soubriquet, could be quite so devastating.

It is in the first scenes of *Purgatorio* that we begin to find the corrective or cure for this infernal malaise, for this odd tendency of signifiers to collapse into signifieds, for words to become things. Dante never lets us forget that what is being purified in the experience of his poem is not only souls but also language, the means by which the soul and its workings become manifest. To purify the language of the tribe, that is, our shared speech, to the point where it becomes once again an adequate instrument for representing the invisible development of the soul toward God is a primary goal of what Dante will call in *Paradiso* his *poema sacro* (*Par.* 25.1).

It happens that one of the pilgrim's and Vergil's first experiences in Purgatory is hearing the singing of the souls in the bark piloted by an angel to the shore of the mountain (*Purg.* 2.37–48). Their song is Psalm 114 and Dante gives us only the first half of the first verse in the Latin of the Vulgate, *In exitu Israel de Aegypto*, but assures us that the souls sang "the rest of that psalm as it is written" (2.48). The complete verse of Psalm 114 reads in the words of the Vulgate:

> In exitu Israel de Aegypto,
> domus Jacob de populo barbaro

> When Israel went forth from Egypt,
> the house of Jacob from a people of strange
> language.[22]

It is well known thanks to the work of Charles S. Singleton that an important part of the meaning of this passage and of the episode in which it is partially quoted in the *Commedia* rests on an established and respected tradition of biblical interpretation whereby the events of the Old Testament were shown to fore-shadow the events of the New.[23] The meaning of the exodus from Egypt was commonly said to foreshadow the turning of the in-dividual soul from sin and confusion (Egypt) to God and salvation (the Promised Land).[24] Beatrice is availing herself of precisely the same tradition when she says to St. James in *Paradiso* 25 of Dante that it is "granted him to come from Egypt to Jerusalem, that he may see, before his term of warfare is completed" (55–57), that is, he has been allowed to make the journey from earth to Heaven, or from the very pit of Hell to the light of the Heavenly City. When we rejoin Vergil and the pilgrim on the shore of Purgatory, we see that they have indeed come from Egypt, the place of corruption, and moreover, as we have been stressing, from "a people of strange language."

But almost more important than *what* the psalm means in

these first scenes in Purgatory is *how* it means with all that is implicit about how it came to mean this. Unlike Guido da Montefeltro's words, which, as we have seen, rest on an attempt to appropriate meaning for the self, to make a kind of raid on meaning, the biblical language of *Purgatorio* with the venerable tradition of interpretation that supports it is the living work of a cultural and historical consensus, not the dead artifact of an individual's corrupted will. What happens in this episode of *Purgatorio* is that, instead of words becoming things, things and events become once again words, the things and events of Old Testament history are shown to speak of the New Testament, they point beyond the specific events that they relate to the presence of God. The word is restored to the public domain, a fact that the chorus of souls singing in unison strongly suggests. The content of their song, the exodus of the Jews from bondage, reminds us of the shared experience of our humanity, whether we see that experience as an arduous journey through a desert from an actual place of slavery to a place of freedom and light, from Egypt to the Promised Land, or as an inward journey, far more a change of mind than a change of place, from confusion and suffering to clarity and joy. The contrast with Guido da Montefeltro's heated efforts to appropriate a shared sacred vocabulary for private ends could not be starker. In and through the biblical passage and the tradition of interpretation with which it is associated language regains the currency that it loses as it passes through the private realm of the diseased imagination and corrupt will.

At this point we must return to that tradition of purgation and education in which, as we have seen, Dante was concerned to locate his poem. All things in Dante's world can be understood as expressions of the spirit of informing love or desire. He is at great pains to remind us that even the damned in Hell (in fact, especially the damned in Hell) are expressing desires. We recall

what Vergil tells the pilgrim about the crowd of souls they see
at the bank of Acheron in *Inferno* 3:

> "e pronti sono a trapassar lo rio,
>   ché la divina giustizia li sprona,
>   sì che la tema si volve in disio."
>
> (124–26)

> "and they are eager to cross the stream, for Divine Justice so spurs
> them that their fear is changed to desire."

The desire of the damned has of course stopped short of its proper
goal, which is to become one with God; it is deformed and stunted
as a result, it permanently lacks what it needs to make its bearers
complete and itself fulfilled. But those who are still in life and
those who have died in penitence can still turn or redirect their
desires, which may well have been headed more or less in the
direction of the desires of the damned, to other things. The word
"conversion" derives from a Latin word meaning simply "to turn,"
"to turn around." The process of purgation as Dante understands
it is thus not a voiding of desire, but a freeing of desire from its
fixation on lesser good so that it may be reinvested in greater,
more complete good.

Desire for Dante is closely connected with the question of
language that we have been examining. Beatrice says to Vergil
in the second canto of the poem, "amor mi mosse, che mi fa
parlare" ("Love moved me and makes me speak" [*Inf.* 2.72]).
She means more than that her love for Dante has made her speak
to Vergil in this instance. Speech is a function of desire in a more
general way as well, because we speak what we lack, through
speech we try to make present what is absent. In this sense we
can talk about Dante's poetic diction as a language of representation, that is, re-presentation, a language that tries to present
or make present again what is felt to be lacking. Dante is at one
with Plato in his understanding of desire as arising from incom-

pleteness (according to Socrates in the *Symposium* one of Love's parents is Poverty) and language is the most important means we have of making our incompleteness known and trying to overcome it.[25] But just as the process of purgation in the *Commedia* is a redirection of desire, a freeing of it from lesser goods, the purgation of language is a freeing of words from partiality too, a reformation of deformed language, a purification of contaminated speech. To come forth from the place of twisted love which is Hell is also, as we have seen, to come forth from "a people of strange language."

It so happens that the second canto of *Purgatorio* contains a particularly striking example of the purification of strange language, of what we might call Dante's habit of recycling words, of purifying them and returning them to usefulness. The pilgrim and Vergil are standing on the shore watching the approach of the heavenly boat with its angel pilot. The Italian text contains a surprise, for the word that Dante uses for the angel pilot is *galeotto* (*Purg.* 2.27), apparently the name, here deprived of its capital letter, of the pander in the Lancelot romance that has been the undoing of Paolo and Francesca ("Galeotto fu 'l libro e chi lo scrisse" [*Inf.* 5.137]). In fact the two words are not historically the same: the name *Galeotto* is simply the Italian version of the original French name of the pander in the romance, Gallehault, while the word *galeotto* comes from the Italian word *galea*, our word "galley," a boat driven with oars, and means the one in charge of a galley, the pilot of such a craft. Dante may have mistakenly believed that the two words were etymologically connected, but whether he did or not, the question we must ask is the same: Why did he use this rather specialized term for a boatman or pilot here when his usual word for such a figure, *nocchiero*, would certainly have done as well? The answer may well be that he is dramatizing for us the process of purifying language, showing us that depriving a word of a contaminating context is a way of freeing it for use in the service of other, broader meanings. By effacing the context he has also removed the stubborn meaning of pander from which the name refuses to budge as long as it remains part of the Lancelot romance. It is here cleansed of its charge of erotic significance and put back into service as a word that refers, of all things, to an angel of God. The word has been installed in a whole new world: instead of being connected with erotic passion, it is now connected with that purified divine love that Dante will call *carità* of which erotic passion is only an aspect.[26] The word seems admirably suited to dramatize the process of purgation, which as we have seen is but a turning and redirection of desire.

It is something of a surprise to find this sort of thing in Dante, but if this localized salvaging operation in language seems peculiar or trivial, it is well to remember that a precisely analogous maneuver is executed at the top of the purgatorial mountain in the key episode of the disappearance of Vergil. The pilgrim's last words to Vergil are nothing but a translation into Italian of a phrase from the *Aeneid*: "conosco i segni de l'antica fiamma" (*Purg.* 30.48) ("I know the tokens of the ancient flame"), a very nearly literal rendering of Vergil's "agnosco veteris vestigia flammae" (*Aen.* 4.23). The pilgrim in his translation is referring to his love for Beatrice, which is far loftier than any merely sexual desire. But Vergil's line *does* refer exclusively to erotic passion: it is Dido who speaks the line in the *Aeneid*, and she is speaking of her awakened erotic feeling for Aeneas, a visitation of the same feeling she has had for her husband Sychaeus. Dante is here performing an operation on a whole phrase similar to the one he has performed on a single word from the Lancelot romance: he picks the phrase out of its original fictional context, empties it of its exclusively erotic meaning, and confers upon it an enormously broadened significance. The phrase has been purified, saved for use, by being redirected toward higher things.

Dante surely transcends Vergil here in the very moment of the latter's return to Limbo, and yet he manages to preserve the sense of continuity between ancient poetry and his own new style. The predecessor is surely kept at a distance at the same time he is required to yield up his riches. We must remember that nothing is ever wasted in Dante's world, although much is necessarily incomplete without the notion of an all-embracing God who confers on all things their final significance. The conspicuous quotation of a Vergilian text at the moment of Vergil's disappearance is in fact a way of suggesting the ground against which the figure of Dante's meaning emerges. Certainly the sexual passion to which the original Vergilian lines exclusively refer is part, though a tragically incomplete part, of the love of which the pilgrim is speaking at the top of the mountain, the love that, as Dante says at the end of *Paradiso* "moves the sun and other stars." Dante does not exclude meanings, he rather incorporates and transcends them, gives fuller significance, just as the tradition in which he participates does not deny instinct, but rather turns it to its proper use, refines and sublimates it to make it function in spiritual projects. Vergil knew of a sexual love that transcends pure passion in that it is directed at procreation. Beyond that, he knew of the multiple senses of *pietas*, that love that orders the life of the family that sexual love generates and in its yet more general meaning of "respectful reverence" makes cities, communities of men on earth, possible. Of Dante's *carità* he has remained ignorant in life, and hence his exclusion from the Heavenly City and the beatific vision with which Dante's poem concludes. He remains to the end just what Statius has said he is, "like one who goes by night and carries the light behind him and profits not himself, but makes those wise who follow him" (*Purg.* 22.67–69).

To recirculate words and fictions in the manner of Dante is precisely to give them a history, or to restore a history which they have lost, to open them to the pressures of use from which the misguided imagination has tried to shield them. To translate Vergil at the moment of his disappearance is perhaps to act out the sense of the Italian pun *traduttore-traditore*, the translator, the betrayer. It is certainly to say that, although the *Aeneid* may have been a personal dead-end for its author, it has made a future possible for others. It is also to remain consistent with the conditions under which Vergil has presented himself to the pilgrim in the Dark Wood, where, as we have seen, he seems voluntarily to introduce himself as a historical being and rigorously refuses to speak as anything else.[27] Dante knew after all that his own Italian word for translator, *traduttore*, means in etymological fact "one who leads across." And to lead across is to salvage from the chaos of history what is valuable, whether it be the words of the *Aeneid* (if not the author of those words), which are given a radically new meaning in the text of the *Commedia*, or the very souls which that text is designed to save. The poem is a sort of boat, as Dante many times asserts, the poet himself a *galeotto* in the purified sense of helmsman, leader, guide—he who leads us across from a people of strange language to "a people just and sane" (*Par.* 31.39), and from a love that is incomplete to that universal love that "moves the sun and other stars."

4   BEYOND THE CLASSICAL TRADITION

If Vergil disappears from Dante's poem and is not led across to the vision of eternal bliss that forms the poem's final canticle, the traces of his technique, the things that the pilgrim has internalized in the course of the first two canticles in his association with Vergil, certainly are and continue to operate with full effect throughout *Paradiso*, though it is an effect that is now distinctly Dante's and no longer Vergil's. The technique of effacing the name, which we have seen Vergil, and Dante after him, practicing, is still very much a part of the diction of *Paradiso*. "Cesare fui e son Iustinïano" ("I was Caesar, and am Justinian" [*Par.* 6.10]), speaks in its very terseness of a moving reversal of the mind from ambition to humility, a reversal that Justinian's subsequent narrative of the history of the Roman Empire confirms by his refusal to name the emperors who have borne the standard, instead promoting the standard itself, the repeated "it" of the story, to the status of hero:

> "Da indi scese folgorando a Iuba;
>   onde si volse nel vostro occidente,
>   ove sentia la pompeana tuba.
> Di quel che fé col baiulo seguente,
>   Bruto con Cassio ne l'inferno latra,
>   e Modena e Perugia fu dolente.
> Piangene ancor la trista Cleopatra,
>   che, fuggendoli innanzi, dal colubro
>   la morte prese subitana e atra.
> Con costui corse infino al lito rubro;
>   con costui puose il mondo in tanta pace,
>   che fu serrato a Giano il suo delubro."
>
>   (70–81)

"From there it fell like lightning on Juba, then turned toward your west, where it heard Pompey's trumpet. Of what it wrought with the succeeding marshall, Brutus and Cassius howl in Hell, and Modena and Perugia were doleful. Because of it sad Cleopatra is still weeping who, fleeing before it, took from the viper sudden and black death. With him it coursed far as the Red Sea Shore; with him it set the world in such peace that Janus's temple was locked."

Modern readers tend to become fidgety before passages like this, and *Paradiso* in particular is full of them. We desperately scan the footnotes trying to discover *who*, in the name of mercy, is being referred to. We can scarcely even identify the points at which the standard changes hands: it is as if runners in a relay race had stepped into a convenient phonebooth to pass the baton. It is true, Dante has posted some signs, "the succeeding marshall," for instance, but is not this shift obscured by the following reference to Brutus and Cassius? We automatically associate the names of Brutus and Cassius with *Julius* Caesar, and they are surely in Hell and perhaps howling because of their betrayal of him. But this "succeeding marshall" must of course be Augustus, and we discover that Justinian is speaking of the *defeat* of Brutus and Cassius at Phillipi (the absent antecedent of "what" in the phrase "what it wrought") and they howl of that. And might Brutus and Cassius be said to howl at an even broader "what"? They are, after all, the enemies of the empire in a very general way as well; might they be howling at *all* the standard wrought with its succeeding marshall, including that profound peace at the birth of Christ? It is no better with names. "It fell like lightning on Juba." Is this a person or a place? A person, to be sure, the Numidian ally of Pompey. Modena and Perugia "were doleful." People might be said to be doleful, but these are of course places, the former near the place of Antony's defeat, the latter the place of his brother Lucius's defeat.

Our confusion is nevertheless part of the point. The names to which so much glamour and prestige naturally attach—Julius Caesar, Augustus Caesar—are consciously suppressed so that we, who are less sure of our Roman history, have to scribble in the margins what has been so carefully eliminated from the text. In Justinian's speech history gets spun out fine in a series of verbs ("It fell . . . turned . . . heard. . . . wrought"), personality gets absorbed in action, and at least the illusion of a sort of rarefied history is created, which in its transparency reveals the Divine Providence that moves in it and through it and gives it being. This is why in the third line of this canto Justinian calls Aeneas, the founder of Roman history, "l'antico che Lavina tolse" ("the ancient who took Lavinia to wife"): that Divine Love, here expressed as the love of a woman in hope of a future race, is what is behind this difficult account of the Roman Empire. The promotion of the "it" of the standard is a way of effacing earthly prestige, of deglamorizing the personality, of restoring the essence of earthly action to which the glamour of names has blinded us.[28]

Justinian's speech is also highly allusive. Some of it is taken from ancient historiography, some from the *Pharsalia* of Lucan, and occasionally we can hear an apocalyptic murmur, a brief "forewhispering" of the loud cries for the vengeance of God which will be central to later portions of the canticle: "who, fleeing before it, took from the viper sudden and black death." But considered as a specimen of a particular kind of style, we can perhaps understand Justinian's speech as Dante's farewell to one of the most conspicuous and durable features of the epic tradition in which he was working, the heroic catalogue. The bluster of this sort of traditional epic set-piece is part of our enjoyment of it, the mouth-filling names and place names, the recital of high deeds, the lavish descriptions of armor and equipment, are all ways of celebrating the stature of the heroes, their gorgeous physical presence, their prowess in battle—all ways, in short, of contributing to their fame, the only immortality, after all, that is available to them. But Justinian for the most part names the *enemies* of the Roman empire, many of whom we have already met in Hell: the lees of history settle out, leaving the transparent fluid in which we can discern the workings of Providence. Insofar as Justinian's speech is a catalogue at all it is a sort of rogue's gallery, a nosology, rather than a celebration of the people it names. Dante has really done something like stand the heroic catalogue on its head, rearranged its traditional emphases, redirected its meaning. And this is not surprising: we are, as we read Justinian's speech, approaching a vision of complete bliss and peace where man's immortal soul becomes one with God. If one of the purposes of the traditional epic catalogue is to contribute to the immortality-in-fame of the heroes it describes, it must necessarily be in a state of becoming obsolete, of fading in the presence of the idea of an absolute personal immortality that is at the heart of Dante's conception of Christian salvation.

All this is to say that the pilgrim's homage to Vergil does not obscure the fact that the poet was perfectly aware that his own poetry extended and broadened the ancient tradition and took it into areas of human experience that the ancients themselves could have scarcely imagined. Dante's attitude toward antiquity is remarkable in that it is deeply respectful without being in the least servile. His capacity for making fine moral discriminations works just as well when he scrutinizes the remnants of classical antiquity as it does when he considers the chaos of his own time. There is not a trace in his poetry of sentimental praise for the good old days, in spite of his reverence for antiquity and his conviction of the degeneracy of his own times. This is why *Inferno* is rich in situations where the classical past is placed in dialogue with the present, made to argue it out on its own inherent merits. We find Sinon, the greatest liar of antiquity, engaged in an ignoble squabble with Master Adam, the notorious counterfeiter of the florin in Dante's own day (30); the hero Jason walks the same ditch with Venedico Caccianemico, the Bolognese pander (18); and Ulysses and Diomedes, to whom Vergil must speak, because as he says they are Greeks and would disdain the pilgrim's merely Italian words,[29] must share their ditch with Guido da Montefeltro.

Dante then refuses to confer prestige on the ancient simply because it is ancient: there is, remarkably enough, no confusion in his mind between the old and the sacred. His saints are, as

often as not, of his own generation or shortly before it (Bona-
venture, Francis, Dominic), his sinners often as old as Jason and
Ulysses. Mere temporal priority makes no special claims upon
his imagination. What counts is the moral quality of the life
lived, not when it was lived, and, although an authentic temporal
destiny, the life of man as it is guided among ethical choices in
the gritty world of passions, parties, and politics, is of great
importance, the place of souls in the otherworld is determined
by moral principles, which are fundamentally atemporal and ahistorical, have been in effect since the Creation, and will continue
in effect until the end in the Last Judgment. This is an uncom-
promising position and one with which we are perhaps not entirely
comfortable, partly because we are all more or less heirs of the
Renaissance, which did evince a propensity for ruin-worship, for
exalting the ancient because it was old. But we will search the
Commedia in vain, for example, for a thoroughgoing and admiring
description of the architecture of ancient Rome. What comes to
mind as an example of ancient building in the *Commedia* is significantly a moldering burial ground, the ancient cemetery at
Arles to which Dante compares the physical layout of the circle
of the heretics (*Inf.* 9.112–17). Surely Dante must have been
aware of the ruined splendor of the Coliseum, the Forum, the
Pantheon, even if these monuments were as yet unexcavated and
obscured by an accumulation of soil. The absence of such things
in his poem can only be accounted for by his deliberate exclusion
of them and his corresponding inclusion of a mere piece of ancient
utilitarian building—a cemetery, and this not even a cemetery
at Rome, but an apparently altogether ordinary cemetery in a
relatively unimportant town in Provence.[30]

This kind of decentering operation, the relegation of the glory
that was Rome to the provinces, is characteristic of Dante's
method in the *Commedia* and helps to explain perhaps even such

basic matters as his preference for the vernacular over the privileged and respected academic Latin of his day. For Dante understood Rome to mean something far more than the city that existed and still exists at the mouth of the Tiber: it is ideally far more a structure of ideas and attitudes than a structure of monumental stones, a city built and rebuilt to music, in poetry, a concept that poets have always grasped more perfectly than architects and those who employ them, perhaps because poets must work not with the physical presence of things, but with language, which is always trying to capture and embody absent ideas and concepts. We recall in this context how many times in *Inferno* the furniture of contemporary Rome, the physical scene, is called upon to clarify an infernal landscape. How big was the giant Nimrod's head? It appeared to Dante "as long and huge as the pine cone of St. Peter's at Rome" (*Inf.* 31.58–59). This apparently innocent and casual reference is actually a rich juncture: "the pine cone of St. Peter's," a huge brass sculpture, seems originally to have been a pagan artifact, said to have stood near the Campus Martius and to have been removed by Pope Symmachus to the old basilica of St. Peter's sometime between A.D. 498 and 512.[31] In Dante's comparison the monumental appears as the monstrous, for as usual he manages to tell us as much about the vehicle as he does about the tenor. We can look through either end of a Dantesque simile and learn something. The tenor here is Nimrod, founder, so Dante believed, of Babel, the anti-city of peoples of strange, mutually unintelligible languages, the ultimate locus of human disorder.

The implication about Rome, the physical city that pride has created, is as clear here as it is when Dante compares the circulation of panders and seducers in the first ditch of Malebolge to the traffic pattern devised by the Roman authorities under Boniface VIII for the Jubilee in 1300:

dal mezzo in qua ci venien verso'l volto,
di là con noi, ma con passi maggiori,
come i Roman per l'essercito molto,
l'anno del giubileo, su per lo ponte
hanno a passar la gente modo colto,
che da l'un lato tutti hanno la fronte
verso 'l castello e vanno a Santo Pietro,
da l'altra sponda vanno verso 'l monte.

(*Inf.* 18.26–33)

on our side of the middle they came facing us, and, on the other side, along with us, but with greater strides: thus the Romans, because of the great throng, in the year of the Jubilee, have taken measures for the people to pass over the bridge, so that on one side all face toward the Castle and go to St. Peter's, and on the other they go toward the Mount.

So much not only for the impressive roll of names—the Castle, St. Peter's, the Mount—but also for the efficacy of Boniface's Plenary Indulgence when taken, as both Boniface, who declared it, and the throngs, who accepted it, seem to have done, as a kind of magic formula that would automatically absolve from sin. The simile is there to do far more than tell us "more clearly how the people looked," for it tells us as well where these people are headed; it says that the people who regarded the indulgence as a kind of automatic absolution divorced from any concern with right willing already have one foot in Hell.

It also tells us that Boniface, mentioned by name in the next canto among the simonists, is a seducer as well, a seducer of multitudes, and that is perhaps one reason why Dante uses a clearly sexual metaphor to describe simony:

O Simon mago, o miseri seguaci
che le cose di Dio, che di bontate

deon essere spose, e voi rapaci
per oro e per argento avolterate.

(19.1–4)

O Simon Magus! O you his wretched followers that, rapacious,
prostitute for gold and silver the things of God which ought to
be the brides of righteousness!

And in this light Dante's curious defense of himself in the same
canto for breaking one of the fonts in St. John's in Florence in
order to save "one who was drowning in it" (19–21) is something
more than a personal reference. Dante, at least, knows the ultimate value of the stones of the church; although he calls the
building "mio bel San Giovanni" (17), he knows that its physical
beauty must not be allowed to quench a life trapped within it.
To break the stones of the church is in this instance to value them
rightly, to see that they point beyond themselves to human and
divine values. Only the simonist with his concern for the stones
as mere matter would call this sacrilege. To break stone is sometimes to return it to history, reinvest it in process. This is what
the unnamed Florentine suicide at the end of *Inferno* 13 (139–
51) cannot understand: instead of seeing the fragmented statue
of Mars at the head of the Ponte Vecchio as historically broken
stone, he sees it as a protective totem, understands only what is
still present, rather than what is absent:

"I' fui de la città che nel Batista
mutò 'l primo padrone; ond' ei per questo
sempre con l'arte sua la farà trista;
e se no fosse che 'n sul passo d'Arno
rimane ancor di lui alcuna vista,
que' cittadin che poi la rifondarno
sovra 'l cener che d'Attila rimase,
avrebber fatto lavorare indarno.
Io fei gibetto a me de le mie case."

"I was of the city that changed her first patron for the Baptist, on which account he with his art will ever make her sorrowful; and were it not that at the passage of the Arno some semblance of him still remains, those citizens who afterwards rebuilt it on the ashes left by Attila would have labored in vain. I made me a gibbet of my own house."

The breaking of stone is an important motif in the *Commedia* simply because Dante realizes that sculpture and architecture are always forms of language, always in a sense texts, like the reliefs he finds on the Terrace of Pride in Purgatory which he calls *visibile parlare*, "visible speech" (*Purg.* 10.95). Like actual texts, and in fact more than actual texts, stone sculpture and architecture have a way of bullying the mind into stopping short of ultimate meaning, of calling attention to themselves as *objects* (from Latin *obiectum*, that which has been thrown in the way): they are literally and etymologically *obvious*, they block the path. Words have perhaps less of a tendency to do this, because it is part of their very nature to mean, but we have seen a whole series of attempts to appropriate words beginning with the text of the *Aeneid*, to turn them into things, to make them point only to the self. This is why neither the figure of Vergil nor the text of the *Aeneid* escapes the consequences of Dante's refusal to accord mere temporal priority the privilege of unquestioned authority, and why Vergil himself is curiously drawn into the process of demystifying himself, his book, the culture from which that book springs, and the later culture, which has attempted to appropriate it in the service of idiosyncratic concerns. For to make a mere text, the product of a human imagination, sacrosanct would be finally as culpable a confusion of sacred and profane as Boniface's attempt to move in the other direction, that is, to secularize the sacrosanct, to take symbols out of circulation. In the *Commedia* deliberate profanation of what has come to be regarded as sacred can be an exemplary act, paradoxically an act of complete piety.

We can see most clearly this process of exemplary profanation in the canto of the diviners and soothsayers (*Inf.* 20), where Vergil is made to correct his own text and, in the process, to call it and himself into question as infallible authorities. The remarkable excursus on the founding and naming of Vergil's native place (*Inf.* 20.58–99) is in fact a recantation of the account that Vergil has given in the *Aeneid* (10.198–203), where he says that Mantua was founded by one Ocnus, the son of Manto and a Tuscan river, and named after Ocnus's prophetic ("fate-speaking," *fatidica*) mother. The Manto mentioned in *Inferno* 20 as the founder of Mantua is the daughter of Tiresias of Thebes, and may not be any relation at all to the Manto of the *Aeneid*. The Vergil of the *Commedia* is oblique, but very firm on the point of his own fallibility:

> "Però t'assenno che, se tu mai odi
> originar la mia terra altrimenti,
> la verità nulla menzogna frodi."
> (20.97–99)

"Therefore I charge you, if you ever hear other origin given to my city, let no falsehood defraud the truth."

It is characteristic of the figure of Vergil as we have seen him that he should make no claim to a monopoly of the truth, and should understand so completely the profound ambiguity and danger inherent in any poetic utterance, especially if that utterance is in any way susceptible to being interpreted as prophecy and enshrined as a kind of holy writ. The complexities of truth-telling are amply dramatized in this very canto, for Aruns (20.46), who is damned for his divining, has in fact told the truth about the Roman civil wars and the defeat of Pompey, whereas Vergil by his own oblique admission has inadvertently lied about the founding of his own city, but in another place has told the truth through the mouth of a liar. This must be one reason why Dante includes Eurypylus among the diviners:

> "Quel che da la gota
> porge la barba in su le spalle brune,
> fu—quando Grecia fu di maschi vòta,
> sì ch'a pena rimaser per le cune—
> augure, e diede 'l punto con Calcanta
> in Aulide a tagliar la prima fune.
> Euripilo ebbe nome, e così 'l canta
> l'alta mia tragedìa in alcun loco:
> ben lo sai tu che la sai tutta quanta."
>
> (106–14)

"That one, who from the cheek spreads his beard over his swarthy shoulders, was augur when Greece was left so empty of males that they scarcely remained for the cradles, and with Calchas he gave the moment for cutting the first cable in Aulis. Eurypylus was his name, and thus my high Tragedy sings of him in a certain passage—as you know well, who know the whole of it."

The passage is of course *Aeneid* 2.114–19, squarely embedded in Sinon's speech. The anecdote of Eurypylus emerges as a local truth designed to lend authority to what was, from Vergil's and Dante's point of view, the most vicious lie ever told. The mixture of truth and falsehood in Sinon's speech, represented here through the anecdote of Eurypylus, is designed to make us aware of the complex dangers inherent in any utterance, both to the speaker and his listeners. Even Aruns, who has told the truth and in so doing has furthered the cause of empire, is damned for his speaking.

To discover why Aruns is in Hell we must, as always with Dante, look not merely at the single act (which has a deceptive way of appearing innocent), but primarily at the whole set and tendency of the life of the man who has performed it and at the lives of men who have performed similar ones. We discover in so doing that Dante is meditating in an expanded way in *Inferno* 20 on prophecy in general, a meditation that will have crucial implications for the poem as a whole, since Dante himself, both in his role as pilgrim and in his role as poet, constantly essays to speak prophetically, to deliver judgment, to discern and speak where other men have been content to remain silent.[32] This is a large responsibility that he takes upon himself, one that constantly runs the risk of being confused with the culpable actions of a host of figures he meets in the course of his journey. Yet Dante's poetry is preeminently a poetry of risk, and it is constantly chancing the confusion of crucial concepts in order to arrive at last at finer distinctions.

Perhaps the first thing we notice about the diviners in *Inferno* 20 is how secluded they have made themselves in life. There is Amphiaraus who has foreseen his own death in the war against Thebes and concealed himself to avoid it; Aruns, who has his cave "among the white marbles" in the hills of Luni (46–51); Manto, who has sought out "land in the middle of the fen, untilled and without inhabitants" (83–84); and of those contemporary with Dante, or nearly so, Asdente and the unnamed women, who have all abandoned their proper social roles—shoemaking, sewing, weaving—to practice in solitude the arts of the occult (118–23). This pattern of flight from society is simply another version of the flight from history. In turning from society all the diviners are really turning from the city, from culture, from all that makes communal life possible. The images of secluded spaces are balanced by images of tilth, husbandry, purposeful manual labor: Aruns's isolated cave is in the hills "where grubs the Carrarese who dwells beneath" (47–48), Manto seeks land "untilled," *sanza coltura* (84). Untilled land is always for

Dante a historyless landscape, the appropriate scene of those who have tried to escape the contingent by controlling the future. We recall in this context the Wood of Suicides in *Inferno* 13 which is even harsher and denser than the preferred country of the "wild beasts that hate tilled lands between Cecina and Corneto" (*Inf.* 13.7–9). And this other untilled landscape is also associated with false prophecy, for here are the Harpies "who drove the Trojans from the Strophades with dismal announcement of future ill" (10–12), a dismal announcement, we remember, which was false in the sense that the hunger that was to force the Trojans to eat their tables (*Aen.* 3.253–57) turns out to be altogether benign (*Aen.* 7.107–17).

In this light Vergil's reference at the end of *Inferno* 20 (129) to the Dark Wood of the first canto of the poem (the *selva selvaggia* or "wild wilderness") emerges as something more than casual. For the Dark Wood is, among other things, Dante's own landscape without history, without location in time or space, a straying from the journey of our life.[33] This is perhaps one reason why Vergil, who comes to lead the pilgrim back to history, does not seem to see the she-wolf that is blocking the pilgrim's way up the hill:

> "Ma tu perché ritorni a tanta noia?
>   perché non sali il dilettoso monte
>   ch'è principio e cagion di tutta gioia?"
>   (*Inf.* 1.76–78)

"But you, why do you return to so much woe? Why do you not climb the delectable mountain, the source and cause of every happiness?"

But if Vergil does not see the image as the bewildered pilgrim does, he knows the concept, for we can say with certainty at least this about Vergil's mysterious prophecy of the *Veltro*, that it comprehends the she-wolf as a thing with a history, with a beginning and an end and an earthly career in between:

> "Molti son li animali a cui s'ammoglia,
>   e più saranno ancora, infin che 'l Veltro
> verrà, che la farà morir con doglia."
>
> (100–102)

"Many are the beasts with which she mates, and there will be yet more, until the Hound shall come who will deal her a painful death."

This is the kind of prophecy that does not turn and flee before the contingent, but rather fixes the gaze on the hard facts of earthly life ("Many are the beasts with which she mates, and there will be yet more . . ."); it does not try to coerce the future with a wish, but rather rests content in the hope of happiness and faith in ultimate justice, although it must necessarily remain vague about when these things shall be ("until the Hound shall come . . .").

We can now understand how right Dante was to include in his poem references to his own personal and political difficulties, to his exile, which, according to the chronological fiction observed in the *Commedia*, is still in the future at the time of the journey through the otherworld. For these references to his personal sufferings are not unabsorbed autobiographical gossip, but a means of establishing the authenticity of a prophetic voice, for we are everywhere reminded of the personal costs of speaking out, of the burdens of the prophet, of his lack of honor in his own country. To speak out is to take upon the self a portion of suffering that could be avoided by remaining silent. After describing the utter corruption of the contemporary Church, St. Peter cries to the pilgrim:

> "o buon principio,
> a che vil fine convien che tu caschi!
> Ma l'alta provedenza, che con Scipio
> difese a Roma la gloria del mondo,
> soccorrà tosto, sì com' io concipio;
> e tu, figliuol, che per lo mortal pondo
> ancor giù tornerai, apri la bocca,
> e non asconder quel ch'io non ascondo."
>
> (*Par.* 27.59–66)

"O good beginning, to what vile ending must you fall! But the high Providence, which with Scipio defended for Rome the glory of the world, will succor speedily, as I conceive. And you, my son, who, because of your mortal weight will again return below, open your mouth and do not hide what I hide not."

"Because of your mortal weight": Peter means, of course, "because you still have your body," but the words clearly imply a task imposed and still to be performed, the burden of historical destiny that the pilgrim must yet carry before he can come permanently to the bliss that he is here allowed only to glimpse. One thinks of Aeneas, whose distress at discovering that shades must *return* to history from the Elysian Fields we have already seen (*Aen.* 6.719–21), but also perhaps of what John must have meant when he tells in Revelation of eating the scroll:

> And I took the little scroll from the hand of the angel and ate it; it was sweet as honey in my mouth, but when I had eaten it my stomach was made bitter. And I was told, 'You must again prophesy about many peoples and nations and tongues and kings.'
>
> (10:9–11)

What Dante calls elsewhere "bread of angels" (*Par.* 2.11) is evidently a more complicated, a more crucially ambiguous substance than either the manna in the wilderness or the ambrosia of the ancient gods. The evangelist is also and necessarily the kakangelist, and he calls suffering on himself as well as others.

We notice that Peter speaks of Providence succoring "speedily"—as he conceives. Does this not mitigate the burdened sense of the passage, and imply, both to the pilgrim and to us, that the pilgrim's words when he comes to speak them will have an immediate effect? For this must also be a danger for him who essays to speak prophetically that he will believe his words to have power, that he will be convinced by the tone of authority in his own voice and become deaf to the utterances of others. We have seen how a rhetoric can become a prison, how one can become so thoroughly convinced by one's own eloquence that one mistakes words for what they are trying to represent, treats language as if it were a collection of things rather than a set of gestures that point beyond themselves. It happens that *Paradiso* 27 is rich in defenses against this very tendency, defenses that show that Dante is fully alive to the dangerous ambiguities inherent in prophetic utterance. Dante is as willing to step back from his own poem in order to let us scrutinize it critically as he has been willing to step back from the poems and fictions and languages of others. If we are tempted, for instance, to understand Providence's "speedy" succor of which Peter speaks as being close at hand, we must stress that Peter calls it speedy as *he* conceives it, and he is contemplating it in the mind of God where all times are equally present.

Later on in this same canto Beatrice makes a veiled allusion to the time when justice will be done on earth:

> "Ma prima che gennaio tutto si sverni
> per la centesma ch'è là giù negletta,
> raggeran sì questi cerchi superni,

> che la fortuna che tanto s'aspetta,
> le poppe volgerà u' son le prore,
> sì che la classe correrà diretta."
>
> (27.142–47)

"But before January be all unwintered, because of the hundredth part that is neglected below, these lofty circles shall so shine forth that the storm which has been so long awaited shall turn round the sterns to where the prows are, so that the fleet shall run straight."

A casual reading may well leave the impression that Beatrice is speaking of a rather short period of time, the passing of the month of January, for instance. But the passage refers to an inaccuracy in the Julian calendar (not corrected until 1582) on account of which the solar year was gaining over the standard year at the rate of about one day in a century. By this reckoning January would move completely into spring, be completely "unwintered," in about ninety centuries.[34] "The storm which has been so long awaited" (*already* so long awaited) is hardly imminent. This is much the same kind of effect we noticed in the meeting with Brunetto Latini (*Inf.* 15.49–54) where earthly time, the thirty-five years of the pilgrim's life, was juxtaposed so starkly to the speeded-up, compressed time of the otherworld. In this instance however the effect works against us: we discover with a kind of shock that we cannot measure divine judgment by our earthly standards. The furious impatience of the prophet, who will after all not be on earth to see the event he predicts, is quietly qualified and checked.

Paradiso 27 also happens to contain Dante's last explicit reference to Ulysses (82–83), the false counsellor and the master example in the poem of the corrupting power of speech.[35] The diction here—"il varco / folle d'Ulisse" ("the mad track of Ulysses")—recalls a whole series of warnings and qualifications dis-

tributed throughout the *Commedia*, and not only what Ulysses
himself calls his "mad flight" (*folle volo* [*Inf.* 26.125]), but also
the pilgrim's own hesitation at the beginning of the journey
("temo che la venuta non sia folle" ["I fear that the coming may
be folly"—*Inf.* 2.35]), and his implied reluctance to denounce
the mighty and powerful (e.g., *Inf.* 19.88, where Dante says,
before telling us how he scolded the simonist Pope Nicholas III,
"Io non so s'i' mi fui qui troppo folle" [I do not know if here I
was overbold . . . "]). Certain of the images in Beatrice's de-
nunciation of cupidity in *Paradiso* 27 can hardly be accidental in
this context:

> "Fede e innocenza son reperte
>   solo ne' parvoletti; poi ciascuna
>   pria fugge che le guance sian coperte.
> Tale, balbuzïendo ancor, digiuna,
>   che poi divora, con la lingua sciolta,
>   qualunque cibo per qualunque luna;
> e tal, balbuzïendo, ama e ascolta
>   la madre sua, che, con loquela intera,
>   disïa poi di vederla sepolta."
>
>   (127–35)

"Faith and innocence are found only in little children; then each
flies away before the cheeks are covered. One, so long as he lisps,
keeps the fasts, who afterward, when his tongue is free, devours
any food through any month; and one, while he lisps, loves his
mother and listens to her, who afterward, when his speech is full,
longs to see her buried."

It will not really do to say that Beatrice is asserting here that we
go astray in spite of the fact that we learn to speak, and that as
children we are good even though we have not yet learned to
speak.[36] The harder but more interesting sense of Beatrice's words
is that we go astray *because* we learn to speak. It is language itself

that emerges here as the potential corrupter; it is no longer an instrument of clarification, but a means of bringing guilty desires to bear. The passage stands at the end of a long series of related reflections on the dangers of language and suggests all that has been implicit in the episode of Paolo and Francesca about the blandishments of words and the dangers of reading and writing them, as well as the far more explicit warnings contained in the episode of Ulysses, in the canto of the seducers (*Inf.* 18), or in the curious episode in *Purgatorio* where Arnaut Daniel, the Provençal poet, is made to recant in his native tongue his *passada folor*, his "past folly" and the poetry in which he made it known (*Purg.* 26.140–47). The abrupt shift from Dante's Italian to Arnaut's Provençal has the effect of rendering the verbal medium suddenly opaque, in order to make us aware of it *as* a medium. We are forced to concede that language is not a piece of glass through which we can serenely view an undistorted world, but inevitably a distorting mediation. In the mouth of an obscurantist it can become a destructive weapon.

Simple naivete in such a situation begins to lose its look of innocence. Ignorance of language, like ignorance of the law, can no longer be a valid plea for the man who undertakes a prophetic poem. This is why we find Dante so often attempting to station us outside his own utterances, giving us a place to stand other than the place behind his own shoulder. The acrostic of *Purgatorio* 12.25–60, much condescended to as a piece of medieval literary childishness, is in fact a distancing device, forcing us to move temporarily against the grain of the written text, forcing us to see that we are *reading words*, not seeing a world. The book is given weight so that we become aware of the thing in our hands, the material artifice that can only be an inadequate equivalent for the universe it attempts to encompass. In Dante's final vision of the universe through which he has passed in order to look at God face to face that universe appears as a book:

> Nel suo profondo vidi che s'interna,
>
>   legato con amore in un volume,
>
>   ciò che per l'universo si squaderna:
>
> sustanze et accidenti e lor costume.
>
> (Par. 33.85–88)

In its depth I saw ingathered, bound by love in one single volume, that which is dispersed in leaves throughout the universe: substances and accidents and their relations.[37]

Meanwhile, Dante has just compared the failure of his own memory (also a book, we recall) to the scattering of Sybil's leaves:

> ché quasi tutta cessa
>
>   mia visïone, e ancor mi distilla
>
>   nel core il dolce che nacque da essa.
>
> Così la neve al sol si disigilla;
>
>   così al vento ne le foglie levi
>
>   si perdea la sentenza di Sibilla.
>
> (61–66)

. . . for my vision almost wholly fades away, yet does the sweetness that was born of it still drop within my heart. Thus is the snow unsealed by the sun; thus in the wind, on the light leaves, the Sibyl's oracle was lost.

The poem as a whole and the poet's mind that produced it finally submit, as everything must for Dante, to the winds of history.

III

Milton: Traditions and the

Individual Talent

My favorite among those intimate talks that the God of Israel has with the one man he can count on (and there is usually but one in a given generation) is recorded in the first book of Samuel. The people of Israel, hard pressed by a war with the Philistines which is going rather badly for them, ask the prophet Samuel "to appoint for us a king to govern us like all the nations" (8:5). Samuel meets this momentous request with much reluctance, for, as he reasons, the people of Israel already have a king, and he is called the Lord of Hosts. Why should the unique and chosen people, a people manifestly distinct from all others in the history of the world, want a king to govern them "like all the nations"? There are, to be sure, reasons: the time of crisis seems to demand strong and centralized leadership, a man who can unite the pluralistic tribal system to counter the Philistine threat. But what of the potential costs?

The very institution of kingship seems an invitation to idol worship, and the unique and chosen people have a well-known propensity for that. Can administrative advantage outweigh the risks involved in setting a king over this idol-ridden multitude?

This is a difficult question for a mere man to answer, and accordingly Samuel prays. The Lord God replies wearily but with exquisite regard for Samuel's feelings:

> "Hearken to the voice of the people in all that they say to you; for they have not rejected you, but they have rejected me from being king over them. According to all the deeds they have done to me, from the day I brought them up out of Egypt even to this day, forsaking me and serving other gods, so they are also doing to you. Now then, hearken to their voice; only, you shall solemnly warn them, and show them the ways of the king who shall reign over them." (8:7–9)

Samuel does as bidden. He reads the people a long list of the abuses in which a king may be expected to indulge: "He will take the best of your fields and vineyards and olive orchards and give them to his servants. He will take the tenth of your grain and of your vineyards and give it to his officers and his servants. He will take. . . . " Samuel ends this distressing list with an admonition that will be familiar to every parent who has tried to warn a willful adolescent about a dubious decision to which he seems committed:

> "He will take the tenth of your flocks, and you shall be his slaves. And in that day you will cry out because of your king, whom you have chosen for yourselves; but the Lord will not answer you in that day." (17–18)

We have no way of knowing whether this passage was also a favorite of John Milton, though it is certain that he kept returning to it in his political treatises. But I am willing to hazard the guess that it was much in his mind in the years after the Restoration. For the day had come—and gone again—when the English people had cried out because of their king, and the Lord had not answered, just as Samuel had foretold. It is not, I think, and as is sometimes facilely said, that Milton believed that the Lord had turned his face from the English nation. He had merely fulfilled the word spoken through his prophet. And now that with the restoration of Charles the English people had once more chosen a king for themselves, there was every reason to think that he would fulfill his word again and in the same manner. It is one of the more moving facts of literary history that in the decade of the 1660s Milton cried out neither because of the king nor because of the will of his God. What he did do, among other things, was to write *Paradise Lost*.

With the Restoration Milton had witnessed the inevitable spectacle, however deplorable, of the past being reassumed in the present. I would like to speculate that he pondered deeply in this period Samuel's words "your king, whom you have chosen for yourselves," for Milton's thoroughly historical way of thinking had revealed to him that there is nothing "natural" about the institution of kingship, that it is not the direct creation of God (we have seen, in fact, that the God of Israel is intensely skeptical about it), but rather the invention of men.[1] Long ago, but nevertheless well within the confines of what Milton considered historical time, men *chose* a king, and now, when they cry out against their choice, the Lord will not answer. The whole problem of choice is at the very center of *Paradise Lost*, for it is a poem deeply concerned with the consequences of those choices that are now entailed upon us. In *Paradise Lost* Milton sustains a prolonged meditation on the history of choosing.

There was a period in Milton's career when he was not inclined to see Samuel's message whole, when the heady possibility seemed to exist that men, having long ago chosen a king, could reject that choice and clear the way for a reformed and republican commonwealth. In the prose from the days of the Long Parliament, preeminently in *The Reason of Church Government* (1642), in *The Tenure of Kings and Magistrates* (1649, 1650), and in *Eikonoklastes* (1650), we find a young man supremely impatient with tradition and custom, ready to reestablish government in what he considers its pristine form, and quite convinced that the backslidings of the Presbyterians in the matter of regicide are a local aberration and not the malign forecast of the massive veering about that would produce the Restoration a decade later. Custom in these documents is a "tyrant," tradition "the perpetual cankerworm to eat out God's commandments"; we are warned against the "bold presumption of ordering the worship and service of God after man's will in traditions and ceremonies":

> First, mistrusting to find the autority of their order in the immediat institution of Christ, or his Apostles by the cleer evidence of Scripture, they fly to the carnal supportment of tradition: when we appeal to the Bible, they to the unweildy volumes of tradition. And doe not shame to reject the ordinance of him that is eternal for the pervers iniquity of sixteen hundred years; choosing rather to think truth itself a lyar, then that sixteen ages should be taxt with an error; not considering the general apostasy that was foretold, and the Churches flight into the wilderness.[2]

Tradition in Milton's prose of the 1640s is but vitrified choice, those choices indeed that have been forgotten as such and have been promoted to the status of the Nature of Things. In *The Tenure of Kings and Magistrates* he denounces in essence the tendency to see those institutions that are in fact matters of social consensus with discernible historical origins as the will of God handed down from on high at the Creation. All his formidable learning is mustered to the attack:

It being thus manifest that the power of Kings and Magistrates is nothing else, but what is only derivative, transferr'd and committed to them in trust from the People, to the Common good of them all, in whom the power yet remaines fundamentally, and cannot be tak'n from them, without a violation of thir natural birthright, and seeing that from thence *Aristotle* and the best of Political writers have defin'd King, him who governs to the good and profit of his People, and not for his own ends, it follows from necessary causes, that the Titles of Sov'ran Lord, natural Lord, and the like, are either arrogancies or flatteries, not admitted by the Emperours and Kings of best note, and dislikt by the Church both of Jews, *Isai*. 26.13 and ancient Christians, as appears by *Tertullian* and others.   (C.P.W. 3:202)

Yet Milton ends this triumphant paragraph with an allusion to 1 Samuel 8, the text with which we began. He concedes that "wise authors" have considered the Jews "much inclinable to slavery," "especially since the time they chose a king against the advice and counsel of God." He will recur to the same passage later on in his treatise, when he will prophesy (and the word is not too strong) that God will turn the people from "Mercenary noisemakers" to "the voice of our Supreme Magistracy, calling us to liberty and the flourishing deeds of a reformed Commonwealth":

> with this hope that as God was heretofore angry with the Jews who rejected him and his forme of Goverment to choose a King, so that he will bless us, and be propitious to us who reject a King to make him onely our leader and supreme governour in conformity as neer as may be to his own ancient government.
>
> (C.P.W. 3:236)

"And in that day you will cry out because of your king, whom you have chosen for yourselves; but the Lord will not answer you in *that* day." Milton has simply forgotten in his optimism that the God of Israel has not regarded the election of a king as a reversible choice.[3] In *Paradise Lost* he will remember again.

I THE RELUCTANT SPEAKER

A significant amount of what Milton wrote is presented as being written at great personal cost to the writer. Necessity constantly forces the poet to speak before he is ready or in a manner unsuited to his innermost wishes. The rhetorical force of the posture is clear: if the writer presents himself as reluctant to speak out because he is fully aware of the dangers and price of speaking, and then speaks out anyway, the sense of the urgency of his message will be bound upon his listeners. It is certain that the posture of the reluctant speaker is recurrent in Milton's work. We have the evidence of *Lycidas*, the introduction to the second book of *The Reason of Church Government*, and the invocations of *Paradise Lost* 7 and 9 to name four signal examples. But in spite of the fact of the forgetful enthusiasm in the political treatises we have glanced at, it is less certain that the reluctant speaker is only a posture, an otherwise empty rhetorical ploy. We may believe too readily that Milton actually spoke hastily and only pretended reluctance. It is a modern prejudice to believe that rhetorical efficacy cannot coexist with sincerity. Certainly Milton did not believe this, no more than he believed that political shrewdness was incompatible with genuine religious faith. If he had believed that, a glance at any of the Hebrew prophets would have quickly disabused him of the notion. In any case, it is a matter of historical fact that, though Milton spoke of writing an epic throughout his adulthood, he did not publish such a poem until 1667. "Long choosing and beginning late" is not only a way of establishing the narrator's judicious carefulness. Milton seems really to have been judicious and careful about some things.

Paradise Lost is a poem everywhere marked by the presence of the reluctant speaker, whether he appears in the guise of the narrator in the invocations, of Adam in his measured conversations with our general mother, or of the angels in Heaven and the devils in Hell when in parallel scenes each group is asked to produce a volunteer to carry out similar but antithetical dangerous missions (2.417–26, 3.217–21). I shall perhaps be accused of paradox when I stress the reticence of a poem that is in excess of ten thousand lines long. Yet it remains a fact that *Paradise Lost* is full of significant silence, hesitations, a remarkable diffidence about initiating discourse:

> Hail holy Light, offspring of Heav'n first-born,
> Or of th' Eternal Coeternal beam
> May I express thee unblam'd? since God is Light,
> And never but in unapproached Light
> Dwelt from Eternity, dwelt then in thee,
> Bright effluence of bright essence increate.
> Or hear'st thou rather pure Ethereal stream,
> Whose Fountain who shall tell?   (3.1–8)

These lines dramatize a hesitant picking out of the way (which is anything but a fumbling), an intense scrupulousness about right naming. The Miltonic "or" is not simply a way of cramming the poem with as many names and things as possible, although it contributes mightily to this end. It is the instrument of the poet who contemplates alternatives, who is always before choices that will make a difference: "On the secret top / Of *Oreb*, or of *Sinai* . . . Or if *Sion* Hill / Delight thee more" (1.6–11); "and underneath a bright Sea flow'd / Of Jasper, or of liquid Pearl" (3.518–19); "Whether the Sun predominant in Heav'n / Rise on the Earth, or Earth rise on the Sun" (8.160–61).[4]

Some twenty years ago Northrop Frye remarked "the simultaneous pull in Milton's life between the impulse to get at his poem and finish it and the impulse to leave it until it ripened sufficiently to come by itself." "That the tension was there," Frye continues, "seems certain from the way in which the temptation to premature action remains so central a theme in his poetry."[5] In *Paradiso* 19 Dante describes the fallen Lucifer (*il primo superbo*) as he "who . . . fell unripe through not waiting for light" (46–48). *Paradise Lost* is a poem preeminently concerned with the value of patience, and not only in its explicit references to this virtue, like the narrator's "Patience and Heroic Martyrdom" (9.32), or Michael's exhortation to Adam to add to the example of the Redeemer "Virtue, Patience, Temperance" (12.583—Milton's significant paraphrase of 2 Pet. 1:5–6), but in dozens of implicit examples as well. One thinks in this context, for instance, of Milton's pervasive gradualism, his emphasis on slow process and the "tract of time":

> time may come when men
> With Angels may participate, and find
> No inconvenient Diet, nor too light Fare:
> And from these corporal nutriments perhaps
> Your bodies may at last turn all to spirit,
> Improv'd by tract of time, and wing'd ascend
> Ethereal, as wee, or may at choice
> Here or in Heav'nly Paradises dwell.
>
> (5.493–500)

It is of great importance that in his temptation of Eve, Satan will paraphrase these words of Raphael to our unfallen parents, carefully suppressing all references to process and the tract of time:

And what are Gods that Man may not become
As they, participating God-like food?

$$(9.716-17)$$

That Raphael has circumspectly hinted at a light which Adam
and Eve may gain by patient waiting suggests that Eve's bold
attempt to participate "God-like food" all in a moment is a sin
against patience. The Fall comes, among other reasons, as the
result of Eve's rush to choose. Her act is the archetype of those
choices whose consequences are entailed upon the generations.

What is of interest with regard to the poet as reluctant speaker
is the sudden garrulousness with which Eve is afflicted at the
moment of her fall. The two halves of her speech leading up to
and then away from her rash act (if anything can be said to lead
away from it) together constitute her longest speech in the entire
poem (9.745–79, 795–833). More important than a simple word
count, however, is the fact that this speech is Eve's only recorded
soliloquy. Both halves are couched as an apostrophe to the forbidden fruit, the first a still lingering meditation (the possibility
of right choosing is present up to the very instant of the Fall),
the second a rash and tragic encomium of the fruit's illusory
powers:

Great are thy Virtues, doubtless, best of Fruits,
Though kept from Man, and worthy to be admir'd.

$$(9.745-46)$$

O Sovran, virtuous, precious of all Trees
In Paradise, of operation blest
To Sapience. $(795-97)$

In Eve's address to an insentient object we recognize a type of
demonic discourse which we have come to identify with Satan
himself:

> to thee I call,
> But with no friendly voice, and add thy name
> O Sun, to tell thee how I hate thy beams.
>
> (4.35–37)

> O Earth, how like to Heav'n, if not preferr'd
> More justly, Seat worthier of Gods.
>
> (9.99–100)

> Thoughts, whither have ye led me, with what sweet
> Compulsion thus transported to forget
> What hither brought us.   (473–75)

Soliloquy in *Paradise Lost* always bespeaks a tragic isolation quite incompatible with the unfallen mode of discourse, which is properly dialogue, whether between man and man or man and God. Eve's soliloquy just here at the moment of her transgression has a particularly chilling effect because we must read it against the background of those solemnly decorous dialogues she has repeatedly engaged in with Adam, their opening exchange in 4 (411–91), or their astronomical discussion in the same book (610–88); their discussion of Eve's demonically inspired dream (5.28–128), or even their discussion on the very morning of the Fall (which comes as close as any to being an argument) about the advisability of working apart (9.205–384). Coming from the situation of dialogue, where give and take, the exchange of thoughts, has a way of keeping the imagination in check, we feel the unbridled character of thought in dialogue only with itself, as in Satan's last soliloquy above, addressed literally to his thoughts. We will be in a position to understand, far better than Eve herself, her first address to the forbidden fruit:

> worthy to be admir'd,
> Whose taste, too long forborne, at first assay
> Gave elocution to the mute, and taught

> The Tongue not made for Speech to speak thy
> praise.   (9.746–49)

"The Tongue not made for Speech": Eve refers, of course, to the
serpent's tongue and in general to what she understands as the
magical metamorphosis of the brute into a reasoning creature.
But given what we have already noticed about the normative
reluctance to speak in *Paradise Lost*, the phrase acquires considerable resonance. Eve's own tongue was by no means made to
speak the praises she will shortly utter (and is already beginning
to utter); in uttering those praises she will add one more significant item to the list of ways in which she can be identified with
the serpent.

    As it is with Eve, so it will be with Adam. We shall find him
in the tenth book adopting a mode of discourse in pointed contrast
to the measured words he has addressed to his spouse in his
unfallen condition. The decorous periphrases ("Daughter of God
and Man, immortal *Eve*" [9.291]), which seem aimed at placing
Eve within the context of the whole cosmos, are replaced with
the type of tirade that only a fallen mind will want to call
spontaneous:

> Out of my sight, thou Serpent, that name best
> Befits thee with him leagu'd, thyself as false
> And hateful; nothing wants, but that thy shape,
> Like his, and color Serpentine may show
> Thy inward fraud, to warn all Creatures from thee
> Henceforth.   (10.867–72)

We have had true and innocent spontaneity of speech when Adam
named the animals shortly after his creation (8.343–54). Here
we have a simple fallen outburst which proceeds quite unspon-
taneously from Adam's long soliloquy in 10.720–844, where he
struggles to find both the source of, and an escape from, his

present unhappiness. In this context Eve appears to him as a convenient repository of all the evil that has befallen him, an easy explanation for the current state of things, in short, as a scapegoat. And where his unfallen addresses to his spouse tended to see her metonymically, as a part of a large whole always present to his consciousness ("Sole partner and sole part of all these joys" [4.411]), here he sees her for the first time metaphorically, he *identifies* her with the serpent who has seduced her.

It is important to note that in identifying Eve with the serpent Adam virtually founds a mode of fallen discourse that the narrator in the sequence of his poem has already shown will result in the false mythopoiesis of the heathen world:

> However some tradition they dispers'd
> Among the Heathen of thir purchase got,
> And Fabl'd how the Serpent, whom they call'd
> *Ophion* with *Eurynome*, the wide-
> Encroaching *Eve* perhaps, had first the rule
> Of high *Olympus*, thence by *Saturn* driv'n
> And *Ops*, ere yet *Dictaean Jove* was born.
>
> (10.578–84)

We are justified in seeing Adam's outburst as inaugurating a number of degraded uses of language from false mythmaking to the magical and incantatory techniques implicit in the shift from metonymy to metaphor. We may even glimpse a primitive notion of pollution in his wish that all creatures may shun Eve hereafter to avoid being ensnared by her "hellish falsehood." And what Milton makes clear is that Adam uses these techniques here, just as men will later use the rhetorical techniques which they found, as a means of obscuring the central role of individual choice in the disasters that only seem to be visited on humanity:

O why did God,
Creator wise, that peopl'd highest Heav'n
With Spirits Masculine, create at last
This novelty on Earth, this fair defect
Of Nature, and not fill the World at once
With Men as Angels without Feminine,
Or find some other way to generate
Mankind?   (888–95)

Why did God create woman? The question has a stark answer: Adam himself wished him to (8.364–67).

"Some tradition they dispers'd": in this phrase Milton is explicitly concerned with the link between a mode of speech (always initially a matter of choice) and the founding of erroneous traditions, those vitrified choices whose initial moments have been forgotten or suppressed, so that they have come to be treated as part of the way things are, as *rerum natura*, not *hominum arbitrium*. We have seen Adam lapsing into unhistorical thinking almost simultaneously with the inauguration of history proper in the Fall, suppressing the fact of his own choice in the matter of the creation of woman and flying to magical and metaphorical modes of thought in an attempt to deny his own part in the terrible plight in which mankind is now plunged.

This almost automatic turn from the undeniable sadness of history will recur in both Adam and Eve in the final books of the poem and is certainly one reason why the ministry of Michael is not only necessary but protracted. Here is Adam, for instance, complaining at his imminent expulsion from the garden:

This most afflicts me, that departing hence,
As from his face I shall be hid, depriv'd
His blessed count'nance; here I could frequent,
With worship, place by place where he voutsaf'd
Presence Divine, and to my Sons relate;

On this Mount he appear'd, under this Tree
Stood visible, among these Pines his voice
I heard, here with him at this Fountain talk'd:
So many grateful Altars I would rear
Of grassy Turf, and pile up every Stone
Of lustre from the brook, in memory,
Or monument to Ages, and thereon
Offer sweet smelling Gums and Fruits and Flow'rs.

(11.315–27)

This speech neatly parallels the lament of Eve fifty lines before
it (268–86). It may be questioned, however, whether it represents
an improvement on that lament, for all the touches of paganism
in Eve's language ("these happy Walks and Shades, / Fit haunt
of Gods" [270–71]), for all her gentle animism. Adam's complaint is clearly more concerned with his immediate relation to
God, but the means by which he imagines he can maintain that
relation are dubious. His use of the past tense to describe the
manifestations of God's presence shows that he now considers
them a thing of the past, part of an incipient narrative to be
recounted to his children. A conception of the living Word as it
continues to intervene in history is giving way in Adam's mind
to a conception of words as the dead trace of an order vanished
forever. Those "grateful Altars" that he imagines, along with the
lustrous stones "in memory, / Or monument to Ages" are un-
comfortably reminiscent of the "Stocks and Stones" which all our
fathers are said to have worshipped in Milton's great sonnet on
the Waldensian Massacre.[6] Within *Paradise Lost* we may well be
reminded of "the fruits / Of painful Superstition and blind Zeal"
(3.451–52), or of those pilgrims who "stray'd so far to seek / In
Golgotha him dead, who lives in Heav'n" (476–77), and who
now, the poet assures us, occupy the Paradise of Fools. The words
of Adam's complaint suggest an inchoate idolatry, the implica-

tions of which are more disturbing than the plangent animism
of Eve's lament. Eve's impulse will lead her to worship what is
nonetheless part of God's creation, though assuredly not God
himself. Her impulse is basically metonymic, a substitution of a
part for the whole. Adam's impulse, if left unchecked, would
result in identifying the products of his own hands with divinity,
something Michael will later sternly warn against:

> O that men
> (Canst thou believe?) should be so stupid grown,
> While yet the Patriarch liv'd, who scap'd the Flood,
> As to forsake the living God, and fall
> To worship thir own work in Wood and Stone
> For Gods!   (12.115–20)

Adam's impulse is metaphoric, and metaphor, as we have seen,
has a distressing way of losing its look of figurative comparison
("this is *like* that") and sliding over into an assertion of identity
("this *is* that").

2 METAPHOR, NAMING, AND PRESUMPTION

Metaphor is also not something the poet can hope to do without
in his chosen medium. Of all the genres, epic, with its normally
expansive narrative thrust, perhaps comes closest to dispensing
with metaphor entirely, but language truly free of metaphor (if
such can be conceived) has probably relinquished its title to the
name of poetry.[7]

There must have been for Milton a good deal of anxiety bound
up with this necessity for metaphor. We have just seen the way
the trope is connected with idolatry for his characters, and it is
but one more step to see that it is connected with the fear of
presumption for the poet. The metaphoric utterance always verges
on the magical utterance, and in so doing it assumes the look—

but hardly the efficacy—of the divine fiat. It is intimately related to naming, and naming, as we shall see shortly, can very easily degenerate into a human metaphor (which unfortunately goes unrecognized *as* metaphor) for creating the thing named. Adam's innocent act of naming the animals *is* innocent precisely because it is done in full consciousness of the *prior* act of divine creation. There can be nothing appropriative in the act as long as he remembers the anterior fiat. It is when the anterior fiat fades from memory, is forgotten by history, or is repressed from consciousness that human naming begins to assume the (wholly specious) look of origination and tries to enter the place of the divine fiat which history has forgotten.

The Miltonic narrator, fully conscious of his lateness as a poet, feels particular vulnerability to the repression of history, that collective failure of memory that afflicts not only beliefs and doctrines, but the very figurative language on which the expression of those beliefs and doctrines is founded. When metaphor and naming fall victim to historical forgetting (we have seen how swiftly this happens after the Fall), the poet who indulges in them—and he really has no choice about it *qua* poet—had better do so with something approaching the full and innocent consciousness of the unfallen Adam. He will otherwise run the risk of speaking like Satan, of forgetting origins (Satan's "We know no time when we were not as now" [5.859]), and of crediting his utterances with the power of the "Omnific Word."

It is thus not surprising to find that one of the characteristics of Milton's distinctive brand of poetic seriousness is not that it attempts to eliminate metaphor (that would be in any case a vain attempt), but that it uses metaphor with the utmost caution and precision. Milton is in this, as in everything else, the careful speaker, ever alert to what is potentially demonic in language, never guilty of casualness in his use of tropes. *Paradise Lost* does not offer its metaphors at a discount, and even such language that seems at first sight casual or callow proves to have serious underpinnings:

> Now Morn her rosy steps in th' Eastern Clime
> Advancing, sow'd the Earth with Orient Pearl.
>
> (5.1–2)

Beginning a fresh phase of epic action with a sunrise was scarcely a novel strategy in Milton's day, nor are the "rosy steps" of morn sufficiently different from Homer's "rosy fingers" of dawn to provoke much sense of discovery in the reader. What may catch his eye, if he has not simply dismissed it as a decorative flourish, is that this Miltonic morn "sow'd the Earth with Orient Pearl." Even here we may remain undazzled by the metaphor based, after all, on the familiar sight of the early sun shining on an earth wet with dew. But there is nevertheless an undercurrent of suggestion that may take us back to the narrator's description of "Th' Arch-chemic Sun" producing "Here in the dark so many precious things" (3.609–11); or forward to Raphael's description of the sun "Whose virtue on itself works no effect, / But in the fruitful Earth" (8.95–96); or even to a host of analogous effects, including the narrator's prayer that the celestial light will irradiate his mind and "there plant eyes" (3.53).

We will never know whether Milton believed as a matter of scientific fact in the sun's generative force on the earth. What is important is that the doctrine serves to support the apparently slender metaphor of the sun as a sower of pearl upon the earth in the opening lines of the fifth book. Or perhaps this is to emphasize unduly a relatively tiny passage; let us say, rather, that Milton's modest metaphor participates in a vast complex of analogies that includes at its most extensive the abundantly creative relation of God to his cosmos ("And sow'd with Stars the Heav'n thick as a field" [7.358]), and at its most intensive the intimate operations of divine grace on the individual heart and mind.

Indeed, the two extremes are suggestively juxtaposed in the opening invocation:

> And chiefly Thou O Spirit, that dost prefer
> Before all Temples th' upright heart and pure,
> Instruct me, for Thou know'st; Thou from the first
> Wast present, and with mighty wings outspread
> Dove-like satst brooding on the vast Abyss
> And mad'st it pregnant: What in me is dark
> Illumine. (1.17–23)

This is what I mean by Milton's cautious and precise use of metaphor, and, indeed, cautious precision does not exclude the kind of intricate interconnection suggested above, but rather demands it. In constructing the complex, massively self-coherent network that is the poem as a whole, Milton earns his individual metaphors. He also avoids—and this is the crucial matter—the unfortunate impression that they are puny and altogether unsuccessful imitations of the divinely creative fiat. His metaphors are thus purified of the demonic taint that appears in the speech of the fallen Adam, and Milton establishes an important distinction between his own fallen but intensely self-conscious voice and the voices of the fallen Adam and Eve, indeed of Satan himself.[8] Just how important this distinction is we shall see in our next section.[9] Meanwhile, it is enough to see that not for the poet is the imperious "Out of my sight, thou Serpent." Adam's is a magical use of language, undignified in the words of mere men because reserved exclusively for the Word in the act of creation.

We may, if we choose, call the remarkably dense interconnectedness of *Paradise Lost* a rhetorical device. But if rhetoric is, roughly, the art of creating impressions, it does not necessarily follow that it is the art of creating false impressions. And it is precisely the fear of creating false impressions (which amounts,

as we shall see, to creating false traditions) that we find everywhere
in and at every level of Milton's longest poem. We have already
explored some instances where that fear is implied by the rash
speech acts of the characters, particularly those of the recently
fallen Adam and Eve. But the direct utterances of the narrative
voice, especially in those privileged moments when it is relatively
unencumbered by the requirements of commentary and the generation of narrative, are, if anything, even more eloquent of that
fear.[10] We are constantly aware of the poet's defending himself
from fear, locating himself with respect to other poets or persons
who have been in the position of receiving tidings from on high.
He meditates on the intricacies and dangers of those who are
divinely inspired (or who think they are) and draws from his
expanded meditation his sense of himself, his place in history,
and the complexities of his calling. To get the full breadth of the
Miltonic meditation, it is necessary to quote at length:

> Descend from Heav'n *Urania*, by that name
> If rightly thou art call'd, whose Voice divine
> Following, above th' *Olympian* Hill I soar,
> Above the flight of *Pegasean* wing.
> The meaning, not the Name I call: for thou
> Nor of the Muses nine, nor on the top
> Of old *Olympus* dwell'st, but Heav'nly born,
> Before the Hills appear'd, or Fountain flow'd,
> Thou with Eternal Wisdom didst converse,
> Wisdom thy Sister, and with her didst play
> In presence of th' Almighty Father, pleas'd
> With thy Celestial Song. Up led by thee
> Into the Heav'n of Heav'ns I have presum'd,
> An Earthly Guest, and drawn Empyreal Air,
> Thy temp'ring; with like safety guided down
> Return me to my Native Element:

Lest from this flying Steed unrein'd, (as once
Bellerophon, though from a lower Clime)
Dismounted, on th' *Aleian* Field I fall
Erroneous there to wander and forlorn.
Half yet remains unsung, but narrower bound
Within the visible Diurnal Sphere;
Standing on Earth, not rapt above the Pole,
More safe I Sing with mortal voice, unchang'd
To hoarse or mute, though fall'n on evil days,
On evil days though fall'n, and evil tongues;
In darkness, and with dangers compast round,
And solitude; yet not alone, while thou
Visit'st my slumbers Nightly, or when Morn
Purples the East: still govern thou my Song,
Urania, and fit audience find, though few.
But drive far off the barbarous dissonance
Of *Bacchus* and his Revellers, the Race
Of that wild Rout that tore the *Thracian* Bard
In *Rhodope*, where Woods and Rocks had Ears
To rapture, till the savage clamor drown'd
Both Harp and Voice; nor could the Muse defend
Her Son. So fail not thou, who thee implores:
For thou art Heav'nly, shee an empty dream.
    Say Goddess, what ensu'd when *Raphaël*,
The affable Arch-angel, had forewarn'd
Adam by dire example to beware
Apostasy, by what befell in Heaven
To those Apostates, lest the like befall
In Paradise to *Adam* or his Race.   (7.1–45)

I have overrun Milton's verse paragraph as a reminder that
there are at least three important relationships between an inspirer
and an inspired that he is juggling here at the beginning of Book

7. These are, in historical sequence, the relationship between Raphael and Adam, that between "the Muse" and Orpheus, and that between Urania and the Miltonic narrator. What explains in part the fervent, urgent tone of the narrator's invocation must be his awareness that the first two relationships between inspirer and inspired have been in at least one important respect failures: the pagan muse has failed, as the angelic minister in the chronology of the poem will shortly fail, to keep her charge from death. If Orpheus's muse is "an empty dream," while the narrator's Urania is "Heav'nly," there is still the unsettling awareness that Urania works in sleep as well as wakefulness, visits the narrator's "slumbers Nightly"; in short, she inspires his dreams. It is not finally that the narrator doubts the validity of his inspiration, but that his meditation on his own creative powers continually turns up similarities between his relationship with a muse and other, less happy instances of those who have received tidings from a muse or heavenly messenger. The Miltonic narrator, always the reluctant speaker, is conspicuously unwilling to take his security for granted. His fear of presumption, perhaps the one Satanic quality that he runs the greatest risk of incurring in writing *Paradise Lost*, is clear from his hesitation about naming the Heavenly Muse: "*Urania*, by that name / If rightly thou art call'd." He may well consider the fate of Bellerophon and invoke meanings as opposed to names.

Naming is a solemn act in *Paradise Lost*, one to be undertaken only with the greatest diffidence and circumspection. We have already glanced at the narrator's hesitation about addressing Holy Light at the beginning of Book 3. Here in the invocation to Book 7 he is, if anything, even more tentative. He is concerned to distinguish his muse from the classical muses by asserting her existence before creation ("Before the Hills appear'd, or Fountain flow'd") and thus to remove from her any suspicion of being a mere projection of the human imagination. Here on the verge of narrating the creation of the cosmos he must have a muse who precedes that creation, who is closely akin to the "Omnific Word" whose sounding brings things into existence and does not merely move around things already created as the words of Orpheus are reputed to have done. And, lest the suspicion arise that the narrator aspires to the condition of the Word, he ponders the example of Bellerophon and sees the possibility of his own fall as a fall into a false mythology, of being condemned to wander an imaginary place, the Aleian Field, as if it were real. To aspire to the status of the Word, whose ability to produce out of apparently minuscule cause a huge volume of effect renders itself tempting to poets, is ultimately to become a prisoner of imagination, either one's own or the imaginations of one's predecessors. It is to recapitulate the archetypal rebellious act of Satan when he rises up in Heaven in emulation of the Word; and for either man or angel it is ultimately to settle for that dwindled parody of divine creativity that is technology. Satan and his legions, having at first aspired to the condition of the creative Word, are at last reduced to mere fabricators, of artillery, of monumental buildings, and on earth and in history, through demonically inspired human beings, of idols.

Milton's anxiety about naming never lets him forget the baleful effects that names have come to have in human history. Naming is for Milton the first step in founding a tradition, the act by which men confer on an aspect of the creation an autonomous existence separate from the maker. We have seen how this works in Eve's idolatrous act following the eating of the fruit, and we may understand it more fully when we reflect that for Milton the very institution of idolatry begins in an act of naming, and that men, in renaming the fallen angels, have conferred on them an independent status:

Though of thir Names in heav'nly Records now
Be no memorial, blotted out and ras'd
By thir Rebellion, from the Books of Life.
Nor had they yet among the Sons of *Eve*
Got them new Names, till wand'ring o'er the Earth,
Through God's high sufferance for the trial of man,
By falsities and lies the greatest part
Of Mankind they corrupted to forsake
God thir Creator, and th' invisible
Glory of him that made them, to transform
Oft to the Image of a Brute, adorn'd
With gay Religions full of Pomp and Gold,
And Devils to adore for Deities.   (1.361–73)

Naming that is (metaphorically) confused with creating may simply lead the poet away from the source of his being (the invisible glory of him that made him) into the Satanic delusion that he creates autonomously and out of himself. Indeed, one of the blandishments of tradition is that the glitter of the established and the prestigious may tempt the poet to repeat what appears to be a powerful act of origination, and what is in fact a mere fabrication. This is one of the sources of Milton's extraordinary diffidence about naming, one of the reasons that he is so hesitant about naming Holy Light at the beginning of Book 3 and Urania at the beginning of Book 7. He is wary of imitating a pagan act (there was a Urania among "the Muses nine," he knows), of calling up the same powers the ancients called up—with what consequences we are told in some detail. He is equally wary of inspiring such imitation, which amounts to founding a tradition or perpetuating one already founded.

The all but insoluble problem for the poet, the man who has committed himself to language, is that all utterance *must* be imitative to some degree if it is to be intelligible. How to speak without repeating what has already been spoken, to find words that are not the repository of the error that has marked human history but are still intelligible? The audience of such words had better be fit, and it will certainly be few. But the alternative is unpleasant to contemplate. Not to interrogate language and one's own acts of utterance is to return to the errors that lie embedded in the canonical body of texts known as literary tradition. Naming, imitating, repeating: these are the acts by which men bring our world under the sway of the demonic, as we shall see in the section that follows. We shall further see that repetition and the compulsion to repeat are the definitive marks of those in Hell.

3 THE LOWER DEEP WITHIN THE LOWEST DEEP

Let us admit that the man wary of traditions, alive to their snares and allurements, who calls himself nonetheless an epic poet, presents us with something of a paradox. Of all the genres (with the possible exception of stage comedy) epic is perhaps the most conservative of its forms and procedures, the most dictatorial about what it must include and exclude. Continuity in the history of Western epic is of the essence, and in essaying to write an example of the genre, if one strays very far from its internal requirements, or ignores procedures entailed by its canon, one soon discovers that one is writing something else. Indeed, the argument has been advanced that in writing *Paradise Lost* Milton overstepped the boundaries to the point where he placed his poem outside the tradition it seems to try to sum up. Thus Thomas Greene finds one of the most distinctive qualities of *Paradise Lost* Milton's "separation of energy and human heroism":

> Satan is unquestionably more vital than Adam, but in the end it is clear that he is less heroic—as the poem defines *heroic*. The only real question is whether such a definition, excluding the expansive,

questing impulse of the ego, suppressing vital zest in favor of dogged, self-contained integrity—whether that definition is consonant with one's idea of epic heroism or even of moral elevation. The great paradox of *Paradise Lost* lies in Milton's withholding from his human characters that spacious power which ennobled his own imagination.[11]

I do not propose to answer this question, but the mere fact that it can be asked suggests the problem that Milton faced in distrusting tradition profoundly and then attempting an example of the most tradition bound of all the genres.

For the present it may be enough to notice that, however one may judge Milton's conception of the heroic, it is a conception carried through with remarkable consistency and rigor. Satan's heroism is constantly called into question, undercut, and submitted to the scrutiny of other perspectives. What is impressive about the Milton of *Paradise Lost* is not only his distrust of traditions in general, but his ability to manipulate traditions, to play off one against another, to open up at every step another unsuspected perspective from which to view the immediate moment. To speak of "Milton's style" may be quite as misleading in this context as to speak of Dante's style in the *Commedia*. Indeed, much of what ranks *Paradise Lost* in my mind with the *Commedia* and the *Aeneid* is Milton's achievement not only of polysemous writing, but also of polyphonic writing. *Paradise Lost* is, like its great predecessors in secondary epic, a poem of many voices, and its polyphony assures that one perspective will always be subjected to the scrutiny of another.

We may begin this phase of our argument by looking at the well-known scene at the beginning of the poem where Satan is revealed chained on the burning lake:

> Nine times the Space that measures Day and Night
> To mortal men, hee with his horrid crew

Lay vanquisht, rolling in the fiery Gulf
Confounded though immortal: But his doom
Reserv'd him to more wrath; for now the thought
Both of lost happiness and lasting pain
Torments him; round he throws his baleful eyes
That witness'd huge affliction and dismay
Mixt with obdurate pride and steadfast hate:
At once as far as Angels' ken he views
The dismal Situation waste and wild,
A Dungeon horrible, on all sides round
As one great Furnace flam'd, yet from those flames
No light, but rather darkness visible
Serv'd only to discover sights of woe,
Regions of sorrow, doleful shades, where peace
And rest can never dwell, hope never comes
That comes to all; but torture without end
Still urges, and a fiery Deluge, fed
With ever-burning Sulphur unconsum'd.

(1.50–69)

These lines may at first glance seem to offer nothing remarkable in the way of a vision of Hell in a Christian epic. Eliot criticized them for the lack of sensuous particulars ("darkness visible" troubled him especially), and indeed if we read by the standards of Dante they may seem somewhat thin.[12] Few editions of *Inferno* fail to include a map of Dante's Hell, a map that is very easy to draw, given the explicitness of Dante's description. It is hard to find, on the other hand, an edition of *Paradise Lost* that includes any diagrams of Milton's Hell. Its topography is simply too elusive for such treatment.

But what Milton sacrifices in particularity he regains in a kind of ambiguity and suggestiveness that can take us far in directions that Dante's admirable concreteness never indicates. For without abandoning the idea of a local Hell fixed in time and space ("As far remov'd from God and light of Heav'n / As from the Center thrice to th' utmost Pole" [1.73–74]), Milton nevertheless suggests a Hell that is a region of the mind, the very creation of the corrupted intellect, which will go on tormenting itself wherever it betakes itself in a kind of ghastly parody of the spiritual autonomy to which it aspired in the first place. We note that the "more wrath" for which Satan's doom has reserved him has to do not with ever more ingenious tortures of which he is at present unaware, but with his own thoughts:

> for now the *thought*
> Both of lost happiness and lasting pain
> Torments him.   (Emphasis added)

Satan's "baleful eyes . . . witness'd huge affliction and dismay," and we are left to discover whether he saw affliction and dismay in the others around him, or his eyes expressed—bore witness to—the affliction and dismay within him. Again, part of what he sees in his first survey of Hell are "doleful shades," which may vaguely describe a feature of the infernal landscape, but may just as well refer to his fallen comrades, who are certainly doleful, and who have become in their corruption shades or *umbrae* in the pagan and classical sense. Indeed, there is a steady tendency in the verse of Milton's first two books to transfer epithets appropriate to persons to features of landscape, as here in "Regions of sorrow," or later in the first book in the description of the fiery lake as an "oblivious pool" (266). There may even be a somewhat recondite pun lurking in the phrase "sights of woe" that suggests "sites of woe."[13] It may be said with some justice that what Satan sees as he casts his baleful eyes around the infernal regions is a vast representation of the contents of his own fallen imagination.

One of the last things Satan encounters before leaving Hell to destroy the newly created world is a product of his imagination in a grotesquely literal sense. He confronts his daughter Sin, sprung Athena-like from his head, as something wholly other to him:

> So strange thy outcry, and thy words so strange
> Thou interposest, that my sudden hand
> Prevented spares to tell thee yet by deeds
> What it intends; till first I know of thee,
> What thing thou art, thus double-form'd, and why
> In this infernal Vale first met thou call'st
> Me Father, and that Phantasm call'st my Son?
>
> (2.737–43)

Satan's contempt for what is in fact a part of himself has always pleased irony hunters. But perhaps the irony is somewhat more complicated than is generally assumed, embracing, as it seems to do, not only Satan's swaggering superiority to his progeny, but his assumption of superiority to the place in which he encounters them. "This infernal Vale" is a heroic snort, the phrase of a creature convinced that he is about to leave Hell for a habitation more befitting his dignity. We know, of course, that he will very shortly make a tragic discovery related to this matter of leaving Hell behind:

> Which way I fly is Hell; myself am Hell;
> And in the lowest deep a lower deep
> Still threat'ning to devour me opens wide,
> To which the Hell I suffer seems a Heav'n.
>
> (4.75–78)

This identification of the container with the things it contains is one of Milton's most characteristic and novel effects, and we hear of it in the most varied contexts. It is, for instance, implicit in the Great Council of the second book, when Belial says:

> whence these raging fires
> Will slack'n, if his breath stir not thir flames.
> Our purer essence then will overcome
> Thir noxious vapor, or enur'd not feel,
> Or chang'd at length, and to the place conform'd
> In temper and in nature, will receive
> Familiar the fierce heat, and void of pain.
>
> (2.213–19)

Or again, in Mammon's speech:

> Our torments also may in length of time
> Become our Elements, these piercing Fires
> As soft as now severe, our temper chang'd
> Into their temper.   (274–77)

Mammon's phrase "in length of time" is a demonic parody of Raphael's "tract of time" (5.498) in which Adam and Eve may gradually become all spirit. The fallen angels will gradually become all Hell.

It is this characteristic mingling of place and person that forms the basis for an implicit critique of the pastoral tradition that Milton conducts throughout *Paradise Lost*. Milton's polyphonic style finds room for examples of most of the traditional genres, but the pastoral, resting as it does on the assumption that a change of place can effect a change of attitude, that in going to the country we can become innocent once again, most obviously challenges his theology and psychology. In the postlapsarian world as Milton understands it, the pastoral is apt to appear sentimental and deluded, a distorted after-image of the original pleasure we enjoyed and have now lost forever. Here is Satan, for instance, congratulating the council and preparing to offer himself for the heroic mission to Earth:

Well have you judg'd, well ended long debate,
Synod of Gods, and like to what ye are,
Great things resolv'd, which from the lowest deep
Will once more lift us up, in spite of Fate,
Nearer our ancient Seat; perhaps in view
Of those bright confines, whence with neighboring Arms
And opportune excursion we may chance
Re-enter Heav'n; or else in some mild Zone
Dwell not unvisited of Heav'n's fair Light
Secure, and at the bright'ning Orient beam
Purge off this gloom; the soft delicious Air,
To heal the scar of these corrosive Fires
Shall breathe her balm.   (2.390–402)

The notion that the fallen angels will find peace on earth appears
in a pathetically ironic light when we read it from the perspective
of Satan's first soliloquy (4.75–78). Here he speaks confidently
of being lifted up "from the lowest deep," there of a "lower deep"
within "the lowest deep" that threatens to devour him. He has
made the discovery that a pleasant place can only *increase* his pain,
and that "from the hateful siege of contraries" all good becomes
bane (9.121–23).

So I would read one of Milton's loveliest similes, where he
describes Satan approaching Eve:

As one who long in populous City pent,
Where Houses thick and Sewers annoy the Air,
Forth issuing on a Summer's Morn to breathe
Among the pleasant Villages and Farms
Adjoin'd, from each thing met conceives delight,
The smell of Grain, or tedded Grass, or Kine,
Or Dairy, each rural sight, each rural sound;
If chance with Nymphlike step fair Virgin pass,
What pleasing seem'd, for her now pleases more,

She most, and in her look sums all Delight.
Such Pleasure took the Serpent to behold
This Flow'ry Plat, the sweet recess of *Eve*
Thus early, thus alone; her Heav'nly form
Angelic, but more soft, and Feminine,
Her graceful Innocence, her every Air
Of gesture or least action overaw'd
His Malice, and with rapine sweet bereav'd
His fierceness of the fierce intent it brought:
That space the Evil one abstracted stood
From his own evil, and for the time remain'd
Stupidly good, of enmity disarm'd,
Of guile, of hate, of envy, of revenge.

(9.445–66)

The place and person of Eve render Satan for the moment "stupidly good," which can never be for Milton substantially good, simply because he was incapable of conceiving of goodness apart from reason and intelligence. Goodness is something chosen by its possessor, not something that happens to him. Adam and Eve are not good because Paradise is pleasant; Paradise is pleasant because, and only as long as, they are good. It is the hot Hell within Satan that soon dispels this mood of place.

If the simile embodies a critique of the pastoral genre, a later passage subscribes Milton's farewell to it. I am thinking of the curious simile he uses to describe the angelic guard that descends with Michael to expel Adam and Eve from the garden:

He ceas'd; and th' Archangelic Power prepar'd
For swift descent, with him the Cohort bright
Of watchful Cherubim; four faces each
Had, like a double *Janus*, all thir shape
Spangl'd with eyes more numerous than those
Of *Argus*, and more wakeful than to drowse,

> Charm'd with *Arcadian* Pipe, the Pastoral Reed
> Of *Hermes*, or his opiate rod.   (11.126–33)

The point seems to be less that the eyes of the cherubim exceeded in number the eyes of Argus than that these cherubic eyes will not be subject to the charms of the pastoral pipe. The cohort, after all, will block our attempts to reenter Paradise for evermore; it precludes even the possibility of pastoral, a genre, Milton seems to be saying, that became obsolete at the very time of its founding.[14]

Satan is the founder of the pastoral genre, simply because he is the first creature to be in a position to remember a fullness of being he no longer possesses. He is thus also the founder of nostalgia, that inevitably frustrated longing for a return that can never come about. If nostalgia represents one of the poles between which his nature is always moving, the other is surely defiance, and just as Satanic nostalgia founds pastoral poetry, so Satanic defiance founds heroic poetry. Consider Satan's first utterance in Hell, which is, according to Milton's fictional scheme, among the inaugural words of the heroic idiom:

> If thou beest he; but O how fall'n! how chang'd
> From him, who in the happy Realms of Light
> Cloth'd with transcendent brightness didst outshine
> Myriads though bright.   (1.84–87)

This outcry, which notoriously resists all attempts at grammatical analysis, is well known to echo Aeneas's cry about the shade of Hector (*Aeneid* 2.274), though the Milton of *Paradise Lost* has an uncanny way of making it seem as though Aeneas were echoing Satan rather than the other way around. In any case, Satan's first speech in Hell is a good example of the way his feelings traverse the territory between nostalgia and defiance: he begins with a plangent reminder of "the happy Realms of Light," moves through a gloomy survey of his present situation ("into what Pit thou seest / From what highth fall'n," [1.91–92]), and arrives at the sort of defiant declaration that we tend to think most characteristic of him:

> What though the field be lost?
> All is not lost; the unconquerable Will,
> And study of revenge, immortal hate,
> And courage never to submit or yield:
> And what is else not to be overcome?
>
> (105–9)

But it is not only that the speech begins with an echo of Aeneas, for it is concluded with one as well:

> So spake th' Apostate Angel, though in pain,
> Vaunting aloud, but rackt with deep despair.
>
> (1.125–26)

This is a clear reminiscence of what Vergil says of Aeneas after his speech to his men, when the Trojans have been driven ashore at Carthage (1.208–9). By bracketing Satan's first speech with allusions to the *Aeneid*, by recalling the sadness of that poem, its dwelling on the passing of the age of high heroism and vital individualism, Milton manages to suggest that the epic *begins* with a meditation on its own passing. It has never been about anything but the fading of the grandeur and clarity we perhaps mistakenly see as its most salient characteristics. Like the pastoral, epic is born obsolescent, and the enormous prestige it has enjoyed in the history of Western literature, its pride of place in the hierarchy of Western genres, Milton suggests, are consequences of its involvement from the first with the demonic.

It is the sense that Milton presents traditional heroic poetry as obsolescent from the beginning that leads me to agree with those who see his War in Heaven as heroic parody.[15] It is not just that the episode abounds in images that seem aimed at pushing epic immensity to absurd limits, as when Raphael, using the venerable "great things by small" formula, compares the angelic war to the collision of two planets:

> such as, to set forth
> Great things by small, if Nature's concord broke,
> Among the Constellations war were sprung,
> Two Planets rushing from aspect malign
> Of fiercest opposition in mid Sky,
> Should combat, and thir jarring Spheres confound.
>
> (6.310–15)

These lines are not simply a foreshadowing warning of the distempering of the universal frame that will in fact take place with the Fall, they are also a parodic inflation of the sort of already inflated pretensions of traditional heroic verse, Homeric or otherwise. To call the confounding of planetary spheres a "small" thing is surely to invite skepticism, quite as much as it is to indulge in diction such as this:

> So Hills amid the Air encounter'd Hills
> Hurl'd to and fro with jaculation dire,
> That under ground they fought in dismal shade.
>
> (664–66)

But Satan's invention of artillery is for me central to Milton's parodic strategy. Here he surely thought of Ariosto (as he often thought of that urbane ironist in unlikely moments), and especially of the story he tells in the ninth canto of the *Orlando Furioso* about Cymosco, king of Friesland, and his artillery. Orlando manages to overcome Cymosco, in spite of the unfair advantage the "hollow iron" gives the latter. He asks as reward nothing but the cannon itself, intent on forever hiding it from the sight of man. To this end he throws it overboard on his return journey:

And thus, when of the tidesway he was clear,
And in the deepest sea his bark descried,
So that no longer distant signs appear
Of either shore on this or the other side,
He seized the tube, and said: "That cavalier
May never vail through thee his knightly pride,
Nor base be rated with a better foe,
Down with thee to the darkest deep below!"

(9.90)[16]

Orlando sees all too clearly that artillery means the end of the institution of knighthood and attempts (unsuccessfully, as it finally turns out) to keep the game going by suppressing the devilish invention.

Milton's strategy must by now be clear, for by assigning the invention of artillery to the *first* conflict that ever took place, he suggests that heroic warfare and the literature of heroic warfare existed from the beginning under the sign of their own impossibility. Artillery was invented by the devil before all worlds, and what seems later, modern, a comparatively recent development is in fact early; the epic idiom was *never* adequate to things as they are. It had always an impropriety about it, though an occulted one. To Joseph Summers's fine observation about the War in Heaven that "however efficient and even inevitable the traditional means of warfare in the traditional wars, the trust in material means in *this* warfare inevitably limits power,"[17] we might add that, from the divine perspective, trust in material means of warfare, indeed, trust in warfare at all, limits ultimate power absolutely.

For warfare is coercion and thus fundamentally opposed to Milton's commitment to choice and the freedom of the will. Geoffrey Hartman has argued persuasively that as early as "L'Allegro" and "Il Penseroso" Milton made the discovery that "man lives in an easy rather than fearful, and daily rather than extraordinary, intercourse with an ambient spirit world."[18] What this means is that Milton discovered that merriness and melancholy are options, pleasures of the imagination to be indulged (or not) at will. They are not moods by which one is attacked and possessed, but rather states that one chooses and enacts. It seems that something nearly akin to this discovery is played out in the far larger cosmic and moral scheme of *Paradise Lost*, for the notion that one is attacked and possessed by evil is the residue of archaic and primitive modes of representation and at its heart lies the myth that the will of one entity can be forced by the will of another. Out of this type of archaic thinking emerges not only Satan's idea that the mind can be modified by place (the proto-pastoral he proposes in 2.390–402), but also his idea of warfare, which is nothing but the repeated attempt to modify the will of the other, an attempt doomed to failure because it disguises from itself the true nature of warfare as a projection of one's own sinfulness onto the other, a perpetual attempt to locate evil elsewhere. A popular modern analogy of psychoanalysis which holds that the analytic process is like an exorcizing of personal demons is perhaps wanting in that it suppresses the fact that the mind was never possessed in the first place. This the analysand comes to realize, and in realizing it he recovers the liberty to choose himself, sees that he has been choosing himself all along. He realizes that his moods are linguistic and histrionic, postures he adopts in return for a variety of rewards. All of *Paradise Lost*, it may be said, is written against the idea of possession in favor of the idea of the individual confronting a series of choices in liberty. The fallen Satan, on the other hand, must live into eternity with the knowledge that the price of his "liberty" was all too great: he has bought himself a mode of being that consists in nothing but the compulsively repeated attempt to reduce the other to the condition of his own enslavement.

It is not altogether surprising that Milton should turn from warfare and militarism, when, as Thomas Greene has reminded us, his age had become, in contrast to the high Renaissance, ever more sedentary.[19] We may further point out that Milton was also in a peculiarly good position to reflect on the ravages of a civil war which, for all its concomitant dislocations and chaos, had failed to produce the republican commonwealth that its instigators had hoped for. In his later life and retirement he could not but recognize the futility of the military endeavor he had witnessed and abetted in the middle of his career. What is perhaps more surprising is the extent to which Milton allowed these thoughts and concerns to surface in the kind of poem traditionally given to glorifying prowess and military superiority. He did so in an attempt to modify the epic genre, and whether in so doing he ended in writing not the last significant example of epic, but the first (and only) example of something else, is perhaps at last a matter of opinion.

It remains a fact in any case that the violent and defiant in *Paradise Lost* are not merely subversive but are subverted in their turn. The by now classical account of Satan's "degradation" in the course of the action seems part of the turn from military matters to the more cerebral and inward action that is at the center of the poem. We need not follow C. S. Lewis all the way to describing the later Satan as "a thing that peers in . . . windows,"[20] but it is certain that the heroic pageantry of which the first two books are impressively full is only that, and that even as Satan has marshalled his troops from off the burning lake and the "horrid front" is engaging in a series of defiant gestures, he is already talking of the "better part. . . . To work in close design, by fraud or guile / What force effected not" (1.645–47). And many of Satan's most impressive moments are undermined by later ones that seem to mirror them and form an implicit critique of them. Where Satan seems most impressive, as when, I have always thought, he confronts the angelic guard in Paradise and demands to contend "Best with the best, the Sender not the sent, / Or all at once" (4.851–52), he will later, in private, seem the more pusillanimous:

> Then let me not let pass
> Occasion which now smiles, behold alone
> The Woman, opportune to all attempts,
> Her Husband, for I view far round, not nigh,
> Whose higher intellectual more I shun,
> And strength, of courage haughty, and of limb
> Heroic built.   (9.479–85)

But ultimately Milton's turning away from warfare and prowess in *Paradise Lost* may be attributed to the pervasive distrust of traditions which we have been examining. His need to remake and revise, to render everything that he took from earlier poetry peculiarly his own, is not so much the sign of an inflated ego or a hypertrophy of the competitive instincts as it is a fear of losing autonomy, of becoming the creature of the tradition in which he was working. We misunderstand him when we see *Paradise Lost* simply as a bid to overgo or outdo his predecessors in the tradition, emphasizing the occasional snarl ("thus they relate, / Erring . . ." [1.746–47]) and paying no attention to the evidence of certain deeply human fears that the poem contains. Again, any tradition begins in conscious choosing, however obscure this fact becomes in the course of time, and the freedom to choose is a human burden difficult enough without the subtle promptings of traditions. Indeed, to follow a tradition may seem to the chooser the result of a deliberative process of conscious choice, but it always runs the risk of delivering the self over to the fossilized choices of history, promoted, over time and through an apparently perennial tendency of the human mind, to the status of the natural. At this point the chooser loses the title to the name and

becomes embroiled in a process of repeating the errors of those
who have gone before him.

It should be stressed that Milton's anxieties in these matters
are creative anxieties, as well as anxieties about being led astray
from the right religious path. Perhaps for a man of his sensibilities
these amount to much the same thing. They are general throughout Milton's work, and though we have already seen something
of them in the prose (where they emerge chiefly as polemical
hatred), they pervade the poetry as well. Here is an early example:

> What needs my *Shakespeare* for his honor'd Bones
> The labor of an age in piled Stones,
> Or that his hallow'd relics should be hid
> Under a Star-ypointing *Pyramid?*
> Dear son of memory, great heir of Fame,
> What need'st thou such weak witness of thy name?
> Thou in our wonder and astonishment
> Hast built thyself a livelong Monument.
> For whilst to th'shame of slow-endeavoring art,
> Thy easy numbers flow, and that each heart
> Hath from the leaves of thy unvalu'd Book
> Those Delphic lines with deep impression took,
> Then thou our fancy of itself bereaving,
> Dost make us Marble with too much conceiving;
> And so Sepulcher'd in such pomp dost lie,
> That Kings for such a Tomb would wish to die.[21]

These lines, written when Milton was in his early twenties, are
not particularly remarkable for the conceit that a poet's most
enduring monument is erected in the hearts of his later readers.
What is more striking is the way that conceit is developed toward
the end of the poem, where Milton suggests that it is the petrified
hearts of Shakespeare's readers that form the building blocks of
his sepulcher. In spite of the primary encomiastic motive, there

is something rather troubling about the notion of a genius so
powerful that it paralyzes those who come after it, turns them
to inert stone, and makes them serve its glory. One is certainly
justified in suspecting that Milton's feelings about the situation
were not entirely unambivalent.[22]

Though a number of sources for Milton's conceit have been
found in Renaissance poetry,[23] it is tempting to speculate that
two interconnected ancient loci stand ultimately behind it. The
first, at the end of *Odyssey* 11, recounts Odysseus's reason for
beating a hasty retreat from the Land of the Dead:

> "the hordes of the dead men gathered about me
> with inhuman clamor, and green fear took hold of me
> with the thought that proud Persephone might send up
>   against me
> some gorgonish head of a terrible monster up out of
>   Hades."   (632–35)

The second occurs in the *Symposium* and playfully takes up the
first. Socrates is engaging in a mock encomium of Agathon's
speech, just completed.

My dear sir, protested Socrates, what chance have I or anyone of
knowing what to say, after listening to such a flood of eloquence
as that? The opening, I admit, was nothing out of the way, but
when he came to his peroration, why, he held us all spellbound
with the sheer beauty of his diction, while I, personally, was so
mortified when I compare it with the best that I could ever hope
to do, that for two pins I'd have tried to sneak away. Besides, his
speech reminded me so strongly of that master of rhetoric, Gorgias,
that I couldn't help thinking of Odysseus, and his fear that Medusa
would rise from the lower world among the ghosts, and I was
afraid that when Agathon got near the end he would arm his speech

against mine with the Gorgon's head of Gorgias' eloquence, and
strike me dumb as a stone.   (198b–c)[24]

Underlying both instances is the fear of being stopped. Odysseus's
fear, like everything else in his experience, is tied to the physical
and concrete: he is afraid that he will be petrified among the
shades and lose his homecoming. Plato takes the fear and characteristically applies it to the action of thought, rather than to
the action of movement. It is still the fear of losing a homecoming
that troubles him, but here "home" is to be understood as the
soul's proper place in the presence of the forms, beyond the world
of becoming. Gorgiastic rhetoric, Socrates ironically implies,
impedes the soul's return to the world of being, because its
ultimate aim is nothing but to win admiration for the speaker.
To the truth it is opaque. It is to be shunned in favor of a linguistic
instrument that can help us approach truth, and this is of course
the properly dialectical form of the eristic dialogue.

One of the intriguing parallels between this passage in the
Symposium and Milton's slender poem in praise of Shakespeare is
that the latter, like the former, expresses a deep reservation
embedded in language that on the surface appears as an encomium. We may not care to argue that the youthful poet was fully
aware of the contradiction, for we may well experience his lines
as deeply ambivalent rather than as consciously ironic. Perhaps
the distinction scarcely matters in any case. What is important
is that we find Milton early grappling with the problem of poetic
tradition, alive to (if not exactly conscious of) certain dangers for
the poet in the workings of literary history. Those dangers are
certainly analogous to (if not identical with) the dangers of tradition which are repeatedly mentioned in the course of the far
more conscious meditation sustained in Milton's political prose.
In *Paradise Lost* they are close to the heart of Milton's representation of Hell.

The demonic image of what it means to be wholly entangled in irrevocable choices comes at the end of Milton's first great vision of Hell and in his final dismissal of the demonic from the poem in the tenth book. The first of these passages has to do with the fallen angels' activity in the absence of their leader. The verse paragraph (2.506–627), one of the longest in the poem, must be sampled rather than quoted in full:

> Toward the four winds four speedy Cherubim
> Put to thir mouths the sounding Alchymy
> By Herald's voice explain'd: the hollow Abyss
> Heard far and wide, and all the host of Hell
> With deaf'ning shout, return'd them loud acclaim.
> Thence more at ease thir minds and somewhat rais'd
> By false presumptuous hope, the ranged powers
> Disband, and wand'ring, each his several way
> Pursues, as inclination or sad choice
> Leads him perplext, where he may likeliest find
> Truce to his restless thoughts, and entertain
> The irksome hours, till this great Chief return.
>
> (516–27)

The passage as a whole seems in many ways one of the most traditional in *Paradise Lost*. Milton describes heroic games, singing, philosophical talk, the five rivers of Hell straight out of the classical canon, and the alternating tortures of fire and ice that might have been lifted intact from the *Divine Comedy*. The passage almost seems a frantic attempt to include those events mandated by tradition which Milton never got around to in the body of Books 1 and 2. Here he touches all the bases on the dead run.

But as traditional as the passage may seem, it is also a meditation on the baleful consequences of tradition, of having forfeited the power of choice and of being locked into a repetitive cycle. The identification of the fallen angels with the place they now inhabit proceeds relentlessly in Milton's assertion that "the hollow Abyss / Heard far and wide, and all the host of Hell / With deaf'ning shout, return'd them loud acclaim." The abyss heard the trumpets, the dwellers in that abyss responded to them; it is as if Milton were sharing out attributes and actions between container and things contained to adumbrate a proximate fusion which will soon be complete. And the abrupt shift into the present tense at line 523 has a curious effect. It is not entirely adequate to explain this as Milton's use of the "historical present," a well-known dramatic device for making action that happened long ago seem present and vivid.[25] Such shifts may have that effect in Vergil (although Vergil's manipulations of tense and aspect are probably more complicated and interesting than has often been assumed);[26] they may even have such an effect elsewhere in Milton's poetry, or elsewhere in *Paradise Lost*. Here the present tense seems the sign of *continuing* activity. Although the activities of the fallen angels are overtly presented as a segment of time ("The irksome hours, till this great Chief return"), the effect of the present tense is to suggest that the activities are *still* taking place, and that events in Hell are continuing and repetitive rather than segmental and finite:

> Another part in Squadrons and gross Bands,
> On bold adventure to discover wide
> That dismal World, if any Clime perhaps
> Might yield them easier habitation, bend
> Four ways thir flying March, along the Banks
> Of four infernal Rivers that disgorge
> Into the burning Lake thir baleful streams;
> Abhorred *Styx* the flood of deadly hate,
> Sad *Acheron* of sorrow, black and deep;
> *Cocytus*, nam'd of lamentation loud
> Heard on the rueful stream; fierce *Phlegeton*

Whose waves of torrent fire inflame with rage.
Far off from these a slow and silent stream,
Lethe the River of Oblivion rolls
Her wat'ry Labyrinth, whereof who drinks,
Forwith his former state and being forgets,
Forgets both joy and grief, pleasure and pain.
Beyond this flood a frozen Continent
Lies dark and wild, beat with perpetual storms
Of Whirlwind and dire Hail, which on firm land
Thaws not, but gathers heap, and ruin seems
Of ancient pile; all else deep snow and ice,
A gulf profound as that *Serbonian* Bog
Betwixt *Damiata* and Mount *Casius* old,
Where Armies whole have sunk: the parching Air
Burns frore, and cold performs th' effect of Fire.

(2.570–95)

Phlegethon inflamed with rage, Lethe rolled, the air burnt frore when the devils first discovered them. But the present tense tells us that they *still* inflame, roll, and burn, and will continue to do so into eternity. We conclude that the devils still explore as well and always find the same things. Indeed, it is at this point that Milton tells us of "certain revolutions" in which all the damned are made to feel "by turns the bitter change / Of fierce extremes," "frozen round, / Periods of time, thence hurried back to fire" (597–603). One of the true horrors of Hell is that it contains no past, nothing that is over and done with. Accordingly, there is something like mockery in comparing the heap of un-thawed hail to the ruin of an ancient pile. It is an image that suggests the history that Hell can never have.

The background of eternal repetition serves to make Satan's heroic departure on his mission somewhat less unique and trium-phant. It is true that Milton tricks out that departure with all the heroic trappings, tells us of Satan's thoughts "inflam'd of highest design," of his soaring flight "Up to the fiery concave tow'ring high" (2.630, 635). But it is not an accident that Satan is compared to a trading fleet in the simile that follows:

> As when far off at Sea a Fleet descri'd
> Hangs in the Clouds, by *Equinoctial* Winds
> Close sailing from *Bengala*, or the Isles
> Of *Ternate* and *Tidore*, whence Merchants bring
> Thir spicy Drugs: they on the Trading Flood
> Through the wide *Ethiopian* to the Cape
> Ply stemming nightly toward the Pole.
>
> (636–42)

The real pleasure of savoring these names on the tongue should not distract us from the fact that the simile looks both forward and back. It is natural that Milton should see the figure of Satan superimposed on the spice-trading fleet, for it is not only that the fleet is coming from the luxurious East to satisfy our fallen appetites for the exotic, but that it should have to come so far at all. It will be on account of Satan that our spices will be removed far off. The simile makes us feel our dispersal as a race, our remoteness from the original Paradise that contained "In narrow room Nature's whole wealth, yea more" (4.207), and no need for adventurous voyages to procure it.

Nor should we forget that Satan's voyage of discovery recalls the scene in Hell that we have just left. He is part of that action, even though he is removed from it, and his "departure" from Hell, as we have already noted, is not really a departure at all, but an extension of Hell's torments into the terrain of the individual interior. Milton cannily reserved the exploration of the "Squadrons and gross Bands" for the end of the catalogue of demonic activities so that it would abut Satan's departure—which stands revealed as neither heroic nor a departure.

We noted earlier that the catalogue also contains a group of fallen angels who sing:

> Others more mild,
> Retreated in a silent valley, sing
> With notes Angelical to many a Harp
> Thir own Heroic deeds and hapless fall
> By doom of Battle; and complain that Fate
> Free Virtue should enthrall to Force or Chance.
> Thir Song was partial, but the harmony
> (What could it less when Spirits immortal sing?)
> Suspended Hell, and took with ravishment
> The thronging audience.   (2.546–55)

The cessation of pain is of course a temporary illusion, and in writing these lines Milton was perhaps thinking of that moment in the ninth *Iliad* when the embassy comes upon Achilles apart by his tents "delighting his heart in a lyre, clear-sounding" (186), "singing of men's fame" (189).[27] This is one of the very few references to bardic activity in the *Iliad* (the *Odyssey*, on the other hand, is full of them), and it seems probable that Milton welcomed the reminiscence in his own lines, for he knew that the Greek hero's joy was to be just as transient as that of the fallen angels. Song can not really "suspend" Hell, no more than Orpheus could ultimately bring back Eurydice from the dead, no more than Achilles' delight in a lyre could prevent the death of Patroklos.

But there is a good deal of Miltonic anxiety in this notion of suspending Hell. It will be noticed that in the lines describing the demonic singing quoted above Milton shifts once again to the past tense, abandoning temporarily the present which is the sign of continuing activity. The effect seems indeed to suspend Hell, to suggest that these things happened once and uniquely and were finished. It is only when the narrative is resumed in the present tense with the description of the exploring parties (2.570ff.) that we realize that Milton's narrative has imitated the effect of the demonic singing it has been describing. This is one of the clearest instances in the poem where Milton reveals his uneasy awareness of the proximity of poetic discourse to demonic discourse. Perhaps the proximity consists in a tendency of both to "freeze" processes, to take something that is either an open-ended evolution (like the spiritualizing process Raphael mentions to Adam and Eve), or a closed cyclic repetition (like the demonic activity in Hell), and render it as static and finished. Many of the peculiarities of Milton's prosody—the long sentences, the extended verse paragraph, the heavy use of enjambment, even the lack of rhyme—may be understood as techniques for resisting the imposition of pattern, ways of overrunning the boundaries that the demons of finiteness in verse are always trying to draw. To suspend Hell is to deny its continuing relevance to the present, to push it back into a distanced realm of fable, rather in the way Adam after the Fall speaks of God's presence to man in the past tense, as something that happened "in those days," but is now over and done with.[28]

It should be obvious that all of Milton's narrative effort in the first two books is directed against suspension. What the poet resists above all is rendering Hell as stasis, giving us a comfortable sense of distance from it. To do this would be, to borrow a phrase from Marvell's dedicatory verses to *Paradise Lost*, to ruin the sacred truths to fable and old song,[29] and it is something for which the epic tradition provides abundant precedent. One thinks of the tradition of an idyllic otherworld, Vergil's Elysian Fields or Dante's Limbo with its groups of philosophers and poets soberly discussing their subjects into eternity. One group of Milton's fallen angels seems to emerge from this tradition and to comment on it:

> Others apart sat on a Hill retir'd,
> In thoughts more elevate, and reason'd high
> Of Providence, Foreknowledge, Will, and Fate,
> Fixt Fate, Free will, Foreknowledge absolute,
> And found no end, in wand'ring mazes lost.
>   (2.557–61)

This we might call the pastoral of death (it is equally the death of pastoral), and Milton terms it "a pleasing sorcery" which can "charm / Pain for a while, or anguish, and excite / Fallacious hope"; but it is nothing but a very temporary anodyne. Hell is not stasis, it is an eternal repetition; to render it otherwise is to succumb to that paralysis we have seen the youthful poet apparently succumbing to, but in fact fending off, in his lines on Shakespeare. The mature Milton's particular brand of making it new seems to consist in making it fluid, of rendering as process that which has become, through the force of tradition and humanity's propensity for sloth, monumental or fixed. There is throughout *Paradise Lost*, as there is throughout Dante's *Commedia*, a rooted hostility to the monumental in all its forms. Milton's sensibility seems markedly to favor the asymmetrical and the organic, the forms of nature as opposed to the forms of architecture, in short, the bower in Paradise as opposed to the Tower of Babel or the Temple of Solomon. At the beginning of his poem he invokes the spirit who prefers "Before all Temples th' upright heart and pure" (1.18); it is after the completion of the Temple that Solomon falls into uxoriousness and idolatry; Pandaemonium is a monument to demonic energy and defiance, and has even been said to recall in some detail St. Peter's at Rome.[30] Against the image of the tower the counterimage of the bower is always asserting itself, and one of the deeply saddening aspects of the "subjected Plain" on which Adam and Eve walk hand in hand in the poem's concluding image is that it seems a place without those recesses and nooks, umbrageous grots and bowers that characterize our first home. We know by the end of the poem that the plain will be the locus of many towers.

To insist on a return to the bower while denying that fallen human history takes place under the sign of the tower would of course be to indulge that pastoral nostalgia that, as we have already seen, Milton regularly presents as futility. Isolating bower and tower is not to charge Milton with the kind of sentimentality he so deeply resists, but simply to point out the opposition as an organizing device. The tower is associated with empire building, with rigid social hierarchy and repressive secular authority, in short, with the phases of history we are even now experiencing. As early as "L'Allegro" and "Il Penseroso" Milton shows his preference for the bower, and though the pair of poems seems remarkably evenhanded, they come to rest not in the "Tow'red Cities" which are said to please in "L'Allegro" (117—and even there the poet has first found delight in seeing "Towers and Battlements . . . / Bosom'd high in tufted Trees" [77–78]), but in the "Mossy Cell" (169) at the end of "Il Penseroso."[31] But in *Paradise Lost*, whether from disillusionment or mature experience, Milton's patience abides the present while contemplating the future, and in so doing reveals its deep connections with the vision of Scripture. Northrop Frye has recently remarked that "the most important single historical fact about the Old Testament is that the people who produced it were never lucky at the game of empire." "Temporal power," he continues, "was in heathen hands; consequently history became reshaped into a future-directed history, in which the overthrow of the heathen empires and the eventual recognition of Israel's unique historical importance are the main events, though events that are still to come."[32] Milton, because of his constant immersion in Scripture, knew this intuitively, and by the end of his career he knew it too well to wallow in sentimental longing for a *locus amoenus*.

This does not mean, however, that the way of the true visionary can be anything but the resistance to the frozen and the fixed that we have been examining. If you are committed to the idea that the great revolution lies in the future at the end of history, your commitment in the present must be to seeing the historical process working itself out toward that end. For Milton fixation amounts to a betrayal of faith, for it is to accept as perfect and finished what is in fact incomplete and in process. This is precisely the kind of thinking we are shown in Hell. It is, for instance, the way of Mammon:

> This deep world
> Of darkness do we dread? How oft amidst
> Thick clouds and dark doth Heav'n's all-ruling Sire
> Choose to reside, his Glory unobscur'd,
> And with the Majesty of darkness round
> Covers his Throne; from whence deep thunders roar
> Must'ring thir rage, and Heav'n resembles Hell?
> As he our darkness, cannot we his Light
> Imitate when we please? This Desert soil
> Wants not her hidden lustre, Gems and Gold;
> Nor want we skill or art, from whence to raise
> Magnificence; and what can Heav'n show more?
> (2.262–73)

To accept second best is to accept Hell, and what Mammon couches as weak defiance is really that nostalgia that we have seen regularly emerging in the thought of the fallen angels. All monumental building, indeed, all imperialism, is for Milton at bottom an attempt to found the kingdom in the present whose time is in the future. It is an attempt to put a period to history before the fullness of time.

Although, as we have seen, Hell itself and those condemned to it can have no history properly speaking, they can have, and indeed have had, a profound effect on the history of our race. Demonic intervention in human history is recorded repeatedly in the narrative of *Paradise Lost*, and Michael's account of it to Adam in the last two books might be read, were it not for a recurrent saving remnant, as the chronicle of the Devil's perennially successful incursions. In reading the final books we are constantly afflicted with a sense of déjà vu, as if we had seen all this before in another place. Indeed, we have:

> In other part stood one who at the Forge
> Laboring, two massy clods of Iron and Brass
> Had melted (whether found where casual fire
> Had wasted woods on Mountain or in Vale,
> Down to the veins of Earth, thence gliding hot
> To some Cave's mouth, or whether washt by stream
> From underground); the liquid Ore he drain'd
> Into fit moulds prepar'd.   (11.564–71)

> Nigh on the Plain in many cells prepar'd,
> That underneath had veins of liquid fire
> Sluic'd from the Lake, a second multitude
> With wondrous Art founded the massy Ore,
> Severing each kind, and scumm'd the Bullion dross:
> A third as soon had form'd within the ground
> A various mould, and from the boiling cells
> By strange conveyance fill'd each hollow nook.
>
>   (1.700–707)

We note the correspondences are complete down to the fact that both human and demonic metallurgy take place on a plain, for Milton prefaces Adam's vision of Tubal-Cain by saying explicitly, "He look'd and saw a spacious Plain" (11.556). Both the infernal and terrestrial plains are ultimately related to "the subjected Plain" on which Adam and Eve will walk hand in hand after their expulsion from Paradise. It rests with their choice whether

that plain will assume the shape of a purgatory, looking forward
to final redemption, or the shape of the infernal landscape, looking
back to the experience of the fallen angels in the first two books.[33]

Milton's deep sense of the relation between the demonic and
history accounts in part for certain stylistic and rhetorical features
of the first two books, and particularly for the rich variety of
place names and proper names, both classical and biblical, he
contrives to insert in the winding periods of his verse:

> Nor content with such
> Audacious neighborhood, the wisest heart
> Of *Solomon* he led by fraud to build
> His Temple right against the Temple of God
> On that opprobrious Hill, and made his Grove
> The pleasant Valley of *Hinnom, Tophet* thence
> And black *Gehenna* call'd, the Type of Hell.
> (1.399–405)

Here we glimpse the very process of human history and human
landscape taking the infernal impress,[34] and many a simile in the
first two books is there not so much to tell us what Hell looked
like by means of comparing the strange with the familiar, but
to tell us what our world *really* looks like when we allow it to
come under the sway of the demonic. Thus Milton's similes are
often aimed at "defamiliarizing" the world which we have lapsed
into complacently regarding as secure, as in the celebrated comparison of Satan to Leviathan:

> or that Sea-beast
> *Leviathan*, which God of all his works
> Created hugest that swim th' Ocean stream:
> Him haply slumb'ring on the *Norway* foam
> The Pilot of some small night-founder'd Skiff,
> Deeming some Island, oft, as Seamen tell,

> With fixed Anchor in his scaly rind
> Moors by his side under the Lee, while Night
> Invests the Sea, and wished Morn delays.
>
>   (1.200–208)

This little vignette, charming in its way, is also an eerie reminder of the deceptive appearances of fallen nature, of the way destruction lurks even in what appears to be our salvation.

It is also—and this should be strictly noted in our brief survey of earth under the influence of the infernal—a reminder of the way salvation sometimes resides in unlikely places. Milton refuses to tell us whether the whale sounded, taking with him the hapless pilot, or whether the pilot rode out the night, anchored to an immobile creature that might very well serve, as long as it remained immobile, as an island. The simile follows a list of Titans, to whom Satan's bulk is also compared, and it is a signal example of Milton's habit of mixing classical and scriptural allusions. There is yet this difference between the creatures of fable, who never existed, and the creature from the Bible, who did and still does: we know what to expect from Briareus or Typhon, for the creatures of fable are simple embodiments of hatred and rebellion, and they represent a nature untouched by grace. In this they are indistinguishable from their mighty opponent Jove, whose reputation for nobleness and light is rather subverted in *Paradise Lost* by mention of his own rebelliousness and his deplorable patricidal tendencies:

> The *Ionian* Gods, of *Javan's* Issue held
> Gods, yet confest later than Heav'n and Earth
> Thir boasted Parents; *Titan* Heav'n's first born
> With his enormous brood, and birthright
>   seiz'd
> By younger *Saturn*, he from mightier *Jove*

His own and *Rhea's* Son like measure found;
So *Jove* usurping reign'd.   (1.508–14)

But Leviathan is a more complicated creature—a polysemous creature, one wants to say—and, in leaving open the possibility that the pilot did survive the night moored by his side, Milton gives us a highly compressed account of the workings of Providence. And precisely what we get here, treated intensively as a poetic image, we get in the lines that follow treated dilatedly:

> So stretcht out huge in length the Arch-fiend lay
> Chain'd on the burning Lake, nor ever thence
> Had ris'n or heav'd his head, but that the will
> And high permission of all-ruling Heaven
> Left him at large to his own dark designs,
> That with reiterated crimes he might
> Heap on himself damnation, while he sought
> Evil to others, and enrag'd might see
> How all his malice serv'd but to bring forth
> Infinite goodness, grace and mercy shown
> On Man by him seduc't, but on himself
> Treble confusion, wrath and vengeance pour'd.
>   (1.209–20)

These lines recall Beelzebub's fear that God may have left the fallen angels their strength so that they may "do him mightier service as his thralls" (149), and they suggest that the point of the Leviathan simile is not all Satan's malice, but his unwitting role as a bringer of grace. The pilot, after all, *does* find shelter in Leviathan's lee, though we are not told for how long. Satan, unlike the monsters of classical fable, is paradoxically caught up in the goodness of Providence. This suggests a radically unified cosmos as opposed to a dualistic one.

It is an irony central to the providential vision of *Paradise Lost* that Satan's separatist and Manichean ambitions should be constantly reincorporated into the seamless unity of the created cosmos. Perhaps what lies at the center of any theodicy, any justification of the ways of God to man, is the realization that the attempt at rupture and escape, the attempt to shut out the ineluctable fact of the real, only succeeds in reduplicating the condition that the self is attempting to deny. Whether we see this recrudescence of structure in the very attempt to deny it as evidence of that structure's fundamental health or as evidence of repressive tyranny will depend very largely on our view of Satan as a character.

Meanwhile, we are in a position to see the poles of nostalgia and defiance, already identified as the organizing elements of that character, as intimately connected. For both may be understood as arising from the compulsion to repeat, to repossess in all its fullness a lost state of bliss. Although Satan has glimpses of the futility of this longing when he discovers the Hell within him (4.73–78), and again when he experiences "the hateful siege / Of contraries" (9.120–21), we find him in our last vision of Hell recurring to the pastoral lie:

> Thrones, Dominations, Princedoms, Virtues, Powers,
> For in possession such, not only of right,
> I call ye and declare ye now, return'd
> Successful beyond hope, to lead ye forth
> Triumphant out of this infernal Pit
> Abominable, accurst, the house of woe,
> And Dungeon of our Tyrant: Now possess,
> As Lords, a spacious World, to our native Heaven
> Little inferior, by my adventure hard
> With peril great achiev'd.   (10.460–69)

Shortly hereafter Satan and his legions are made to endure the metamorphosis into serpents, and his posture in that state is surely intended to recall the posture in which we have first encountered him, prone on the burning lake:

> His Arms clung to his Ribs, his Legs entwining
> Each other, till supplanted down he fell
> A monstrous Serpent on his Belly prone,
> Reluctant, but in vain.   (512–15)

A metaphor has become literal: in the first book Satan is *like* the Titans, *like* Leviathan, *like* the huge snakes in *Aeneid* 2 ((cf. *Aen.* 2.204–8 with *P.L.* 1.192–95). Here he really *is* a serpent, and we last see him helplessly repeating the condition in which we have found him at first. In spite of all the clangor surrounding his quest, in spite of the numerous analogies that are drawn between his quest and others of the heroic tradition, he has in a very real sense gone no place at all. To be in Hell is for Milton to be in Hell wherever you happen to find yourself.

4 THE COMPULSION TO REPEAT

Freud linked the compulsion to repeat with the subject's attempt to master retrospectively a traumatic experience for which he had been unprepared at the time of its occurrence. The phenomenon, evident in such diverse manifestations as war neuroses and children's play, seemed to Freud to contradict the dominance of the pleasure principle in psychic life in that the subject deliberately returned to the experience of unpleasure in dreams or in the rituals of play and set aside for the moment the pursuit of pleasure, which was otherwise the paramount authority governing his motivation. Ultimately, Freud speculated, the compulsion to repeat was "a universal attribute of the instincts and perhaps of organic life in general." "*It seems, then, that an instinct is a compulsion inherent in organic life to restore an earlier state of things* which the living entity has been obliged to abandon under the pressure of external disturbing forces; that is, it is a kind of organic elasticity, or, to put it another way, the expression of the inertia inherent in organic life." If we ask what this "earlier state of things" which organic life seeks to restore can be, the answer is that it can be nothing but death, that instincts try "to return to the inanimate state." " *'The aim of all life is death.'* "[35]

There is, to be sure, an obvious objection to the notion that the instincts as a whole seek death, and Freud meets it directly:

> The hypothesis of self-preservative instincts, such as we attribute to all living beings, stands in marked opposition to the idea that instinctual life as a whole serves to bring about death. Seen in this light, the theoretical importance of the instincts of self-preservation, of self-assertion, and of mastery greatly diminishes. They are component instincts whose function it is to assure that the organism shall follow its own path to death, and to ward off any possible ways of returning to inorganic existence other than those which are immanent in the organism itself. We have no longer to reckon with the organism's puzzling determination (so hard to fit into any context) to maintain its own existence in the face of every obstacle. What we are left with is the fact that the organism wishes to die only in its own fashion. Thus these guardians of life, too, were originally the myrmidons of death. Hence arises the paradoxical situation that the living organism struggles most energetically against the events (dangers, in fact) which might help it to attain its life's goal rapidly—by a kind of short-circuit. Such behavior is however precisely what characterizes instinctual as contrasted with intelligent activity.[36]

I should not care to overstate analogies, far less to psychoanalyze Milton's text, but it does seem that Freud's account of the instinctual life sheds some light on the paradoxical mingling of nostalgia and defiance which is characteristic of Satan. Defiant separatism, heroic threats, the flourishes of the warrior steadfast in his defeat may be understood as preparing the way for that nostalgia that wills a return to the original fullness, to the prior state of things, and, though in Milton's theology that prior state is not called death but perfect life, we fallen students of *Paradise Lost* have frequently had a tendency to attribute vitality to Satan and to see in Milton's God something rather pale and disappointing. It remains a fact in any case that Satan denies remembering, and the inevitable result of his denial is repetition:

> We know no time when we were not as now;
> Know none before us, self-begot, self-rais'd
> By our own quick'ning power, when fatal course
> Had circl'd his full Orb, the birth mature
> Of this our native Heav'n, Ethereal Sons.
>
> (5.859–63)

Satan's denial of his origins, his assertion that he is self-begotten, can be fairly called repression, and this can only result in the repetition of the repressed material. Again, Hell has no past, and therefore memory is irrelevant there. Satan and his legions, whatever they seem to be doing, can only repeat the attempt to return to origins, they can never remember the wish on which the attempt rests as something belonging to the past.

Perhaps Freud's speculations can illuminate our view of the Miltonic narrator as well, whom we have been characterizing as a reluctant speaker, a man wary of traditions, both those already in place and those that might be founded by his own discourse. It is not too much to say that a fear of tradition may be characterized as a fear of repetition, and that one of the narrator's overriding motivations is to avoid being absorbed by the closed cycle characteristic of his Hell. *Paradise Lost*, we might say, is a poem marked by intelligent, rather than instinctual, effort. Harold Bloom's account of the trope of metalepsis in the poem shows Milton at his uncanny best in avoiding the snares of tradition, at projecting his own lateness in Western literature paradoxically as an earliness, and at making it seem as if all his predecessors were actually quoting *Paradise Lost* rather than the other way around.[37]

I find Bloom's account in general very convincing, though in concluding I should like to express a few reservations based on the final books of the poem. I am a greater admirer of *Paradise Lost* 11 and 12 than many, and what C. S. Lewis called an "unassimilated lump of futurity,"[38] seems to me, on the other hand, quite strictly bound up with the scheme of the poem as a whole, with Milton's fear of repetition, with his scriptural commitment to a future-directed history. It is Adam's fallen tendency to repeat, to relapse into nostalgia (11.315–29), or inappropriate pity or delight (500–514, 598–602) that dictates what has seemed to some the inordinate length of the last two books, far more than any slavish adherence to the historical account found in Scripture. I am not even troubled, though perhaps I should be, by what Thomas Greene calls "Milton's arrogant moral aristocracy," by the standards of which "the community matters less than the salvation of the few."[39] And if, toward the end, Milton's verse loses its well-known sinuousness and obliquity, there is surely a sense in which this is appropriate; the unfallen world must, after all, be difficult for the fallen reader to construe. The final books deal with a world that is all too familiar, and the greater directness of the verse is a style answerable to our familiarity with the fallen.

There is, however, something related to this matter of greater directness that is troubling. It might be called an unseemly explicitness, which amounts at times to a direct attack on the heroic tradition and which seems in its directness to misrepresent it. It is perhaps no accident that Bloom's admirable argument concentrates on the first book and has nothing to say about the poem's conclusion, for surely we miss in the last two books the subtle obliquity of the transumptive techniques in the body of the poem. What Milton has heretofore accomplished with implicit deftness, with resonances of which we are often scarcely aware, is here made a matter of direct statement. As long as Milton's critique of the epic tradition is accomplished through allusions so subtle that they scarcely seem the work of the poet at all, but meanings implicit in his material from the beginning, that critique has the force of inevitability. When we come to a passage like the following, however, we are justified in feeling that something has been extroverted that had better been left implicit, or left aside altogether:

> For in those days Might only shall be admir'd,
> And Valor and Heroic Virtue call'd;
> To overcome in Battle, and subdue
> Nations, and bring home spoils with infinite
> Man-slaughter, shall be held the highest pitch
> Of human Glory, and for Glory done
> Of triumph, to be styl'd great Conquerors,
> Patrons of Mankind, Gods, and Sons of Gods,
> Destroyers rightlier call'd and Plagues of men.
>
> (11.689–97)

Everyone can agree with Milton's admirable sentiments, his hatred of force and imperialism, his love of reason and peaceful persuasion. But the lines go beyond the expression of such unimpeachable sentiments to suggest that the literature that seems to be about warfare is only about that and nothing else.

But it is about something else. One has to squint a good deal to see Milton's lines as a fair characterization of the heroic tradition. If "infinite / Man-slaughter" adequately describes the middle books of the *Iliad*, it tells us nothing of the quiet sublimity of *Iliad* 24. Most of us will want to include in our conception of "Heroic Virtue" Achilles' return of the body of Hector, and we might search all of *Paradise Lost* and not find as moving an example

of a controlled silence as Homer provides in the parley between
the old king and the young warrior:

> But now Priam spoke to him in the words of a suppliant:
> "Achilleus like the gods, remember your father, one who
> is of years like mine, and on the door-sill of old age.
> And they who dwell nearby encompass him and afflict him,
> nor is there anyone to defend him against the wrath, the
>   destruction.
> Yet surely he, when he hears of you and that you are still
>   living,
> is gladdened within his heart and all his days he is
>   hopeful
> that he will see his beloved son come home from the
>   Troad.
> But for me, my destiny was evil. I have had the noblest
> of sons in Troy, but I say not one of them is left me
>   now."   (24.485–94)

Achilles' reply to this is memorable partly because of what he
does not say. To Priam's suggestion of a joyful homecoming
Achilles does not object what he knows very well through the
prophecy of his mother—that he is doomed to die by the walls
of Troy and that there will be no one to defend his father "against
the wrath, the destruction." Achilles' destiny is evil as well, but
instead of insisting on what he knows to be true, he returns a
gesture that abolishes all differences created by what he knows
and what Priam cannot. He feels simply, one speculates, his and
Priam's unity in the uncountable sadness of human life:

> He took the old man's hand and pushed him
> gently away, and the two remembered, as
>   Priam sat huddled

at the feet of Achilleus and wept close for man-
    slaughtering Hektor
and Achilleus wept now for his own father,
    now again
for Patroklos. (508–12)

Achilles, we remember, *is* one of the "Sons of Gods," but his sense of sharing mortality with Priam is perhaps as much a part of his "Heroic Virtue" as the "infinite / Man-slaughter" of his great *aristeia*. The simple fact is that the heroic tradition of warfare contained its antithesis, its own implicit critique, in the earliest examples we have of it. Milton, of course, knew better: his lines are willfully shortsighted, ignoring as they do the nobleness of Achilles, the piety of Aeneas, and a good many other examples from the tradition that provides *Paradise Lost* with a matrix.

It is in the last lines of the poem, admired by nearly everyone but Dr. Bentley, that we can remark a return to the subtle obliquity that characterizes by far the greatest part. In describing the departure of our first parents from Paradise, Milton does seem to close the epic tradition, not by rejecting it out of hand, but by including it in a vision so broad and deep that it seems for a moment to contain all others:

The Cherubim descended; on the ground
Gliding meteorous, as Ev'ning Mist
Ris'n from a River o'er the marish glides,
And gathers ground fast at the Laborer's heel
Homeward returning. High in Front advanc't,
The brandisht Sword of God before them blaz'd
Fierce as a Comet; which with torrid heat,
And vapor as the *Libyan* Air adust,
Began to parch that temperate Clime; whereat
In either hand the hast'ning Angel caught
Our ling'ring Parents, and to th' Eastern Gate

> Led them direct, and down the Cliff as fast
> To the subjected Plain; then disappear'd.
> They looking back, all th' Eastern side beheld
> Of Paradise, so late thir happy seat,
> Wav'd over by that flaming Brand, the Gate
> With dreadful Faces throng'd and fiery Arms:
> Some natural tears they dropp'd, but wip'd them soon;
> The World was all before them, where to choose
> Thir place of rest, and Providence thir guide:
> They hand in hand with wand'ring steps and slow,
> Through *Eden* took thir solitary way.   (12.628–49)

There are any number of things about this extraordinary passage
worth remarking. It seems, for one, perfectly poised between our
first parents' expectation of a bearable and peaceful life and reminders of the Satanic threat to that expectation. We find evidence
of the latter in the image of the evening mist, reminiscent of
Satan in the ninth book "wrapt in mist / Of midnight vapor"
(158–59), or "like a black mist low creeping" (180). But again,
Milton says the mist in our present instance "gathers ground fast
at the Laborer's heel," and we are reminded of the promise that
Eve's seed, though springing from fallen mankind (the laborer
suggests fallen mankind), will triumph over Satan: his heel will
bruise Satan's head.

But I find a low-keyed Vergilian echo the most intriguing
aspect of the passage. Perhaps it is that the view of Paradise as
a "happy seat" is reminiscent of the *beatae sedes* that Aeneas loses
in the course of Vergil's poem and tries to regain. Or perhaps it
is that, as Adam and Eve look back at the happy seat, we are
reminded of the recurrent Vergilian verb *respicere*, the characteristic action of looking back over the shoulder at what is irretriev-
ably lost. As Adam and Eve are led beyond the walls of Paradise,
they look back at what they have forfeited and see "the gate /

With dreadful Faces throng'd and fiery Arms." Those "dreadful Faces" have provoked a great deal of commentary. It has been suggested that Milton availed himself of a tradition that God appointed certain fallen angels to guard Paradise after the expulsion of man, and, more persuasively perhaps, that the phrase is subjective, that to Adam and Eve any angels who are preventing them from returning to the one place they have ever known (at that, the most beautiful place on earth) must appear dreadful.[40]

But there is also a resonance characteristic of Milton. In *Aeneid* 2 the hero is also expelled from the one place he has ever known, walled and sacred like Paradise, and by a heavenly messenger, his mother Venus, who comes to persuade her son that further resistance is futile. Every reader remembers the splendidly conceived scene in which Venus turns her son in various directions, and actually points to the hostile gods laboring at the Fall of Troy:

'hic, ubi disiectas moles avulsaque saxis
saxa vides, mixtoque undantem pulvere fumum,
Neptunus muros magnoque emota tridenti
fundamenta quatit totamque a sedibus urbem
eruit. hic Iuno Scaeas saevissima portas
prima tenet sociumque furens a navibus agmen
ferro accincta vocat.
iam summas arces Tritonia, respice, Pallas
insedit limbo effulgens et Gorgone saeva.'

(2.608–16)

'Look: where you see high masonry thrown down,
Stone torn from stone, with billowing smoke and dust,
Neptune is shaking from their beds the walls
That his great trident pried up, undermining,
Toppling the whole city down. And look:
Juno in all her savagery holds

The Scaean Gates, and raging in steel armor
Calls her allied army from the ships.
Up on the citadel—turn, look—Pallas Tritonia
Couched in a stormcloud, lightening, with her Gorgon!'

(799–808)

In Milton's passage Adam and Eve are also looking back in order
to see the dreadful faces, which, as we can now see, may well
have come from Vergil. Vergil continues, after Venus has warned
Aeneas and disappeared in the thick of night:

'apparent dirae facies inimicaque Troiae
numina magna deum.'   (622–23)

"And now the dire forms appeared to me
Of great immortals, enemies of Troy."

(814–15)

Those *dirae facies* that Aeneas sees may well have suggested the
"dreadful Faces" at the gate of Paradise, although Milton has
arranged the echo to make it seem that his faces came first, that
Vergil based his phrase on Milton's. The episode in the *Aeneid*
may reasonably be taken as the inaugural moment of the poem's
action properly speaking: it is at this instant that Aeneas determines to flee, to submit himself to the unknown sea on a quest
he as yet but dimly comprehends. Milton is of course rather
conspicuously ending his action at the moment Vergil's began.
It was those dreadful faces, Milton seems to say, those first dreadful faces that our first parents saw looking back at Paradise in
the first moment of human history that made it possible for Vergil
to speak of *dirae facies* on the walls of Troy, centuries after the
expulsion from the garden. "All the burial-places of memory give
up their dead." The root of *all* our woe stands revealed.[41]

Conclusion

W E may conclude with a further application of Freud's thought in *Beyond the Pleasure Principle*, a document that has been called with a great deal of justice Freud's "masterplot."[1] For Freud what we call simply "life," the prolongation and elaboration of the self, is in reality a detour, a swerving from the direct path leading to a former state of things, a swerving entailed upon the organism by exterior forces, environmental influences that the organism must take into account if it is to die in its own fashion. In a very deft and suggestive application of Freud's thought to the theory of narrative, Peter Brooks speculates that all narrative is a courting of premature endings, of improper deaths, and that our experience of the narratable rests largely on the tension between the tendency to short-circuit the process of arriving at the appropriate end and the drive to further elaborations that will guarantee that end:

Plot is a kind of arabesque or squiggle toward the end. It is like Corporal Trim's arabesque with his stick in *Tristram Shandy*, retraced by Balzac at the start of *La Peau de chagrin* to indicate the arbitrary, transgressive, gratuitous line of narrative, its deviance from the straight line, the shortest distance between beginning and end—which would be the collapse of one into the other, of life into immediate death.[2]

Thus Scheherezade emerges as the "story of stories,"[3] because her narrative feat is quite literally a prolonged detour, a staving off or evasion of the wrong death, a long way around in order to guarantee her choice of ending. A story, like an organism, it would seem, wishes to die "only in its own fashion."

Freud's description of life as a detour, a roundabout journey to its ultimate goal, seems to recapitulate the epic journeys we have been examining in the course of three chapters, for in Vergil, Dante, and Milton we have repeatedly confronted attempts to beat a direct path to the quiescent end, attempts frustrated by the structure of the quest imposed from without on a hero who is frequently marked more by reluctance than by boldness. In the course of his wanderings Aeneas is again and again tempted by simulacra of his origins, and it is certainly no accident that the regressive episode with Dido is precipitated by an act of narration, Aeneas's repetition of the Fall of Troy and all his subsequent experience. Dido embodies the temptation to repeat, certainly for Aeneas, and, one might speculate, for Vergil himself. The generic status of *Aeneid* 4 is germane here, for, as has often been noticed, the book is full of allusions to Greek tragedy, and the figure of Dido herself shows clear filiation with Euripidean heroines, Medea and Phaedra in particular. Her death is eminently theatrical, for it is not so much suffered as staged and enacted, and it is of the greatest significance that she sees herself in death not just as a shade, but as an image:

vixi et quem dederat cursum fortuna peregi,
et nunc magna mei sub terras ibit imago.

(4.653–54)

"I have lived and accomplished the course fortune gave, and now
a great image of me shall pass beneath the earth" (my translation).
Dido claims precisely to be dying in her own fashion, and perhaps
she is, if we understand suicide as a way of choosing that which
is actually inevitable, of rewriting the baleful decree of Necessity
in one's own personal style.

But Dido's fashion cannot be Aeneas's, nor, we may add, can
Euripides' be Vergil's. There is something distinctly archaic and
obsolete about Dido's tragedy. Perhaps it is simply that ancient
tragedy has a tendency to monumentalize the individual, to fix
him in the form of a great image. It is a reasonable guess that
Vergil experienced this tragic tendency as antithetical to his own
historical commitment. The dead who matter in the *Aeneid* are
not great images; they are the shades who, according to Vergil's
cosmological scheme, will be reincarnated and recirculated and
thus continue to be part of the ongoing historical process. They
bear the character of unfinished narratives, while the great images
in the underworld, of whom Dido is one, are completed stories,
relegated for the rest of time to the regions below. This is why
Dido appears in the sixth book in a group of mythical heroines,
some of whom have been the subject of formal tragedies:

his Phaedram Procrimque locis maestamque Eriphylen
crudelis nati monstrantem vulnera cernit,
Euadnenque et Pasiphaen; his Laodamia
it comes et iuvenis quondam, nunc femina, Caeneus
rursus et in veterem fato revoluta figuram.
inter quas Phoenissa recens a vulnere Dido
errabat silva in magna. (6.445–51)

> He saw here Phaedra, Procris, Eriphyle
> Sadly showing the wounds her hard son gave;
> Evadne and Pasiphae, at whose side
> Laodamia walked, and Caeneus,
> A young man once, a woman now, and turned
> Again by fate into the older form.
> Among them, with her fatal wound still fresh,
> Phoenician Dido wandered the deep wood.
>
> (600–607)

We have already noted that she does not speak to Aeneas because she now exists in a different order of being. It is perhaps not too much to say that she exists in a different literary genre.

The way of the Vergilian hero must be the long way around, the detour, the *longo . . . circuitu* of Helenus's prophecy in the third book (412–13), the "long sail round." This is the necessary deviation, the space opened up for narrative, and it is a deviation no less important to Vergil than to Aeneas. For the poet as well must not allow himself to become entangled in the past, to repeat in an ahistorical manner the ancient genres. He must remain free to end his narrative in his own fashion, and of course the major figure here is Homer, with whom Vergil was sharing a genre.

It is one thing to present nonnarrative genres like drama as archaic within a narrative genre. It is quite another to present an example of the same genre as archaic, and the density of Homeric allusions within the *Aeneid* testifies to Vergil's consistent agonistic endeavor even in what seem like unproblematic minor details. Even a list of names in the *Aeneid*, imported from the Homeric poems, can betray the struggle to lay the ghost to rest. Here is, for instance, the apparently unremarkable description of what Aeneas sees as he gains the *arva ultima* of the first region of the underworld, including the shades who have fallen in the battle for Troy:

hic illi occurit Tydeus, hic inclutus armis
Parthenopaeus et Adrasti pallentis imago,
hic multum fleti ad superos belloque caduci
Dardanidae, quos ille omnis longo ordine cernens
ingemuit, Glaucumque Medontaque
   Thersilochumque,
tris Antenoridas Cererique sacrum Polyboeten,
Idaeumque etiam currus, etiam arma tenentem.

(6.479–85)

Here Tydeus came to meet him, and then came
Parthenopaeus, glorious in arms,
Adrastus then, a pallid shade. Here too
Were Dardans long bewept in the upper air,
Men who had died in the great war. And he groaned
To pick these figures out, in a long file,
Glaucus, Medon, Thersilochus, besides
Antenor's three sons, then the priest of Ceres
Polyboetes, then Idaeus, holding
Still to his warcar, holding his old gear. (643–52)

Parts of the catalogue are lifted whole from Homer. Vergil's "Glaucumque Medontaque Thersilochumque" is nothing but a translation of Homer's "Glaukon te Medonta te Thersilochon te" in *Iliad* 17.216,[4] yet this may be precisely the point. Aeneas doesn't see warriors, he sees, so to speak, a Homeric catalogue of warriors. These fallen comrades from the past are now images who will not return to history. They have come to an end in their own Homeric fashion so that Vergil may come to an end in his.

It may be questioned whether Vergil's technique of foregrounding is entirely successful, whether he did manage to liberate his poetry from the compulsion to repeat the past. One way of reading the enigmatic end of *Aeneid* 6 is, after all, to say that Aeneas's departure from the underworld by the gate of false dreams (898) indicates that he is still a fiction, still caught up in the shadow-world, the first experience of which has also had to do with false dreams:

> In medio ramos annosaque bracchia pandit
> ulmus opaca, ingens, quam sedem Somnia vulgo
> vana tenere ferunt, foliisque sub omnibus haerent.
>
> (6.282–84)

> In the courtyard a shadowy giant elm
> Spreads ancient boughs, her ancient arms where dreams,
> False dreams, the old tale goes, beneath each leaf
> Cling and are numberless.   (386–89)

And at the end of the poem it is difficult to escape the feeling that the enraged hero, "furiis accensus et ira" (12.946), as he slays the suppliant Turnus and accomplishes what amounts to a vendetta, is recapitulating the wrath of Achilles.[5] Somehow the figure of Achilles abides in the *Aeneid*, and, if he is not being represented by Turnus, who is oddly like the Aeneas of most of the poem at the end, he will be represented by Aeneas himself.

What is certain in any case is that Vergil invented, at least for Dante and Milton, and probably for a host of other poets as well, the technique of looking at previous literature in the context of the world of the dead as a means of being able to remember it without having to repeat it. Vergil thus opens the poetic uncon-scious and at least points the way toward the poet's liberation from it. What I think we must always find mildly astonishing about Dante is the apparently serene confidence with which he extends the Vergilian way with regard to Vergil himself. For the *Commedia* is not only full of Vergilian quotation ("allusion" in either case is often not a strong enough term), but the figure of Vergil himself is allowed into the poem, and not, as we have already seen, in the guise of the "Medieval Vergil," but as a carefully restored approximation of the historical figure who wrote the *Aeneid* in the time of the good Augustus. And it is the historical Vergil to whom Dante the pilgrim openly professes allegiance—"fealty" might be the better word—and declares his great original: "Tu se' lo mio maestro e 'l mio autore" (*Inf.* 1.85) ("You are my master and my author"). Dante treats the *Aeneid* quite frankly as a historical document and uses it to demystify any number of persons and texts with historical pretensions, quite as if he had joined with the master as apprentice or junior partner.

One speculates that Dante's palpable openness, his apparently total confidence about revealing authority, is not the result of some putatively medieval naivete, but of the fact of what we have already called his bibliocentric culture. He was, after all, relieved of the necessity of fictionalizing Vergil and the events of the *Aeneid* by his conviction that the Bible constituted ultimate and unimpeachable authority and that his own poem was implicated with the Bible in a way that Vergil's never could be. Where Dante recurs to the notion that Vergil was a prophet of the New Dispensation, as when he has Statius assert that his conversion came as the result of reading the fourth *Eclogue* (*Purg.* 22.73), it is with the express purpose of denying Vergil's knowledge or intention of Christian doctrine. Dante's relatively secure relation to Scripture must continually generate awareness of Vergil's ignorance of it, and the act of introducing the author of the *Aeneid* *in propria persona* into the text of the *Commedia* emerges as an ambivalent gesture, at once of submission and mastery. Thus the *Commedia* is not without reminders of Vergil's exclusion from Revelation, from his plangent exclamation concerning the Heavenly City in the first canto of *Inferno*—"oh felice colui cu' ivi elegge!" (129)—which seems sadly to echo the classical formulae *beatus ille* or *felix qui*, to his return to Limbo in *Purgatorio* 30.

Dante has more oblique reminders as well, and perhaps they are all the more powerful for being oblique. There is a curious contradiction in *Inferno* 31, for instance, where the pilgrim and Vergil approach the brink of the ultimate circle and are finally lowered to its floor by the giant Antaeus. From a distance the giants, who stand around the periphery of the ninth circle and are visible only from the waist up from the level of the eighth, appear to the pilgrim to be huge towers, and accordingly he asks the master "che terra è questa?" (21) ("what city is this?"). Vergil immediately suggests that the pilgrim is in error:

> "Però che tu trascorri
> per le tenebre troppo da la lungi,
> avvien che poi nel maginare abborri.
> Tu vedrai ben, se tu là ti congiungi,
> quanto 'l senso s'inganna di lontano."
>
> (22–26)

"It is because you pierce the darkness from too far off that you stray in your imagining; and when you reach the place you will see plainly how much the sense is deceived by distance."

It is a fact, however, that the pilgrim's mistake returns again and again in the similes of the verses that follow:

> però che, come su la cerchia tonda
> Montereggion di torri si corona,
> così la proda che 'l pozzo circonda
> torreggiavan di mezza la persona
> li orribili giganti, cui minaccia
> Giove del cielo ancora quando tuona.
>
> (40–45)

for, as on its round wall Montereggione crowns itself with towers, so here the horrible giants, whom Jove still threatens from heaven when he thunders, betowered with half their bodies the bank that encompasses the pit.

> Non fu tremoto già tanto rubesto,
>> che scotesse una torre così forte,
>> come Fïalte a scuotersi fu presto.
>>> (106–8)

Never did mighty earthquake shake a tower so violently as Ephialtes forthwith shook himself.

> Qual pare a riguardar la Carisenda
>> sotto 'l chinato, quando un nuvol vada
>> sovr' essa sì, ched ella incontro penda:
>> tal parve Antëo a me che stava a bada
>> di vederlo chinare.   (136–40)

Such as the Garisenda seems to one's view, beneath the leaning side, when a cloud is passing over it against the direction in which it leans, such did Antaeus seem to me as I watched to see him stoop.

The similes, we must take it, are the distinct province of the poet, as opposed to the pilgrim, part of the act of composing the poem after the experience that the poem recounts is complete. They are thus spoken over Vergil's head or beyond his hearing, and the experiential mistake, which it is Vergil's role to correct, returns as poetic truth. For the ninth circle *is* a city in the metaphorical sense that it is a demonic parody of the Heavenly City, and in superimposing the image of the tower on the image of the body, Dante may well have been thinking of a passage from John's message to the Seven Churches:

He who conquers, I will make him a pillar in the temple of my God; never shall he go out of it, and I will write on him the name of my God, and the name of the city of my God, the New Jerusalem which comes down from God out of heaven.   (Rev. 3:12)

In the City of Satan the pillars are not those who have conquered, but those who have been utterly defeated and cast down.

Metaphor, as Walker Percy has reminded us, can be understood as a species of mistake,[6] and in this instance Dante, in passing from pilgrim to poet, has converted his experiential mistake into metaphor by the interposition of a text that Vergil has never read. The pilgrim's fealty to Vergil must always be read in the context of the poet's consciousness of what separates him from Vergil. The Roman poet in *Inferno* is the spokesman for the literal level, the clarifier of knowledge gained through the senses ("you will see plainly how much the sense is deceived by distance"): he has not at his disposal the vast network of typological connections based on Scripture which are in the possession of the fully educated pilgrim, who is Dante the poet writing *post facto* about his experience from the vantage of the beatific vision at the end of *Paradiso*.

Dante does not thus claim temporal priority over Vergil; he simply makes his own lateness seem an enormous advantage. The repeated pathos of Vergil's situation in the *Commedia* may be described as the pathos of earliness, of the man whose death in history has come just short of the New Dispensation, and Dante did not have far to look for that pathos, for it is repeatedly inscribed in the text of the *Aeneid* itself:

> Vix e conspectu Siculae telluris in altum
> vela dabant laeti et spumas salis aere ruebant,
> cum Iuno aeternum servans sub pectore vulnus
> haec secum.   (1.34–37)

> They were all under sail in open water
> With Sicily just out of sight astern,
> Lighthearted as they plowed the whitecapped sea
> With stems of cutting bronze. But never free

Of her eternal inward wound, the goddess
Said to herself.   (50–55)

'ter conatus ibi collo dare bracchia circum;
ter frustra comprensa manus effugit imago,
par levibus ventis volucrique simillima somno.'
                                    (2.792–94)

                    "Three times
I tried to put my arms around her neck,
Three times enfolded nothing, as the wraith
Slipped through my fingers, bodiless as wind,
Or like a flitting dream."   (1028–32)

tendebantque manus ripae ulterioris amore.
                            (6.314)

And reached out longing hands to the far shore.
                            (425)

"Almost, but not quite" might be a Vergilian motto: the poem
is full of fleeting images that are just out of human reach, ad-
umbrating a pattern of poignant frustration which amounts to a
recurrent thwarting of desire. The good, the desirable, the beautiful are always fleeing before the grasp in Vergil's poem, to the
point where life sometimes seems a softened repetition of the
torments of Tartarus:

                    lucent genialibus altis
        aurea fulcra toris, epulaeque ante ora paratae
        regifico luxu; furiarum maxima iuxta
        accubat et manibus prohibet contingere mensas,
        exsurgitque facem attollens atque intonat ore.
                            (6.603–7)

> Golden legs gleam on the feasters' couches,
> Dishes in royal luxury prepared
> Are laid before them—but the oldest Fury
> Crouches near and springs out with her torch,
> Her outcry, if they try to touch the meal.
>
> (808–12)

It is not difficult to believe that Dante saw the repeated frustration in the *Aeneid* as an emblem of Vergil's falling short of the Christian era, a shadowing of the personal tragedy of earliness that informs the figure of Vergil in the *Commedia* from first to last.

We have already seen that Milton uses the *Aeneid* in a related way, but in the service of the more encompassing project of making the epic tradition as a whole seem obsolescent by attaching the earliest moments of it to the Vergilian meditations on the passing of glory and splendor. Milton worries the problem of belatedness a good deal in *Paradise Lost*, and not only in the narrator's meditations on "an age too late, or cold / Climate, or Years" that may prevent his flight to "higher Argument" (9.42–45), but in implicit instances as well. One of the fallen angels' deepest grudges against man is that he is a late-comer, created after the angels, puny in the etymological sense of *puis né* ("born after"):[7]

> here perhaps
> Some advantageous act may be achiev'd
> By sudden onset, either with Hell fire
> To waste his whole Creation, or possess
> All as our own, and drive as we were driven,
> The puny habitants.   (2.362–67)

Beelzebub's sneer can only remind us of what Milton knew with Dante, that temporal priority confers no special privilege and that the ancient is not necessarily admirable because it is old. In

Paradise Lost man's puniness makes him, indeed, the recipient of special grace, and the fact that he repeats the overweening act of Satan in an apparently slavish imitation of the past is the beginning of God's mercy to him:

> The first sort by thir own suggestion fell,
> Self-tempted, self-deprav'd: Man falls deceiv'd
> By th' other first: Man therefore shall find grace,
> The other none.   (3.129–32)

Milton's own sense of being *puis né* led him repeatedly, as Harold Bloom has amply shown, to the trope of metalepsis, a substituting of himself and a few carefully chosen contemporaries for his predecessors in the place of priority. He "crowds" the imagination (the phrase is Dr. Johnson's) with images that are only apparently adventitious:

>   his ponderous shield
> Ethereal temper, massy, large and round,
> Behind him cast; the broad circumference
> Hung on his shoulders like the Moon, whose Orb
> Through Optic Glass the *Tuscan* Artist views
> At Ev'ning from the top of *Fesole*,
> Or in *Valdarno*, to descry new Lands,
> Rivers or Mountains in her spotty Globe.
>   (1.284–91)

Galileo makes an appearance here, not casually or because some mistaken hankering for plenitude has run amok but as a reminder of the contemporary poet's superior vision:

> Homer and Spenser emphasize the moonlike brightness and shining of the shields of Achilles and Radigund; Milton emphasizes size, shape, weight as the common feature of Satan's shield and the moon, for Milton's post-Galilean moon is more of a world and less

of a light. Milton and Galileo are *late*, yet they see more, and
more significantly, than Homer and Spenser, who were early. Milton gives his readers the light, yet also the true dimensions and
features of reality, even though Milton, like the Tuscan artist,
must work on while compassed around by experiential darkness in
a world of woe.[8]

We might add to this admirable account that Milton's comparison manages to stir into life memories of certain archaic
notions of the heavenly bodies as gods or malign supernatural
powers. "The broad circumference / Hung on his shoulders like
the Moon" flickers with the suggestion of Satan as a lunar Atlas,
a dark world-supporter, until the empirical curiosity of the Tuscan
artist utterly demystifies the notion and relegates it to fable and
folklore. Another burial-place of the memory gives up its dead,
and not only is Satan once again revealed as the Father of Lies,
but Milton manages to suggest the error of another large imaginative tradition and to disentangle himself definitively from
it. He has escaped the malign lunar influence in several senses,
and, while the lunar image will recur in Book 1 in sinister
contexts, associated with the pagan goddess Astarte (438–41),
and as an opponent of the sun in a solar eclipse causing evil
influence (594–99), it is with an image of the moon as "arbitress"
that the first book draws toward a close:

> or Faery Elves,
> Whose midnight Revels, by a Forest side
> Or Fountain some belated Peasant sees,
> Or dreams he sees, while over-head the Moon
> Sits Arbitress, and nearer to the Earth
> Wheels her pale course. (1.781–86)

Milton's lovely image also has its burial-places and its dead to
yield up, and among them we should not be surprised to find

Vergil. The peasant's hesitation (he "sees / Or dreams he sees")
reminds us once again of Aeneas's somber meeting with Dido in
the mourning fields of Book 6:

> quam Troius heros
> ut primum iuxta stetit agnovitque per umbras
> obscuram, qualem primo qui surgere mense
> aut videt aut vidisse putat per nubila lunam.
>
> (6.451–54)

> The Trojan captain paused nearby and knew
> Her dim form in the dark, as one who sees,
> Early in the month, or thinks to have seen, the moon
> Rising through cloud, all dim. (608–11)

The significant difference, to be sure, is that Milton has replaced
Vergil's heroic history-bearer with an unnamed peasant, an un-
specified representative of humankind, rather like the laborer who
makes a brief appearance in the final lines of *Paradise Lost*. His
refusal to name the peasant is not only an effective way of undermining the aristocratic pretensions of the fallen angels as they
sit in council. It seems to purge the heroic tradition of its aristocratic ideology as well. Milton's democratic feelings, a good
deal muted in comparison to the days of the Long Parliament,
are nevertheless still vigorously present in his greatest poem.

It would seem that Milton achieves something like the
"sprightly port" of Shakespeare's Antony here. For all the unnamed peasant's anonymity, he is, like the laborer in the last
lines of the poem, or the pilot of the night-foundered skiff, or
even "the *American* . . . girt / With feather'd Cincture" (9.1116–
17), whom Columbus encountered in the New World, an ex-
emplar of all our race, not of just a part of it. His struggle—the
interior debate of choices—is our struggle until the end of time,
and, whether we choose to deem it more or less heroic than wars

and military prowess, Milton has succeeded, if at times uneasily, in making it stand out vividly against the high heroics of Hell. In the brief appearances of his unnamed representatives of humanity—peasant, laborer, pilot, American—Milton universalizes his themes and makes them ours. What Shakespeare accomplished with stunning *sprezzatura*, Milton, rather more characteristically than is often supposed, accomplishes with his silent but richly meaningful representatives.

Paradise Lost ended the epic tradition in English poetry. That is a fact, but what remains problematic is whether in writing it Milton simply succumbed to certain seismic rumblings in the social and cultural bedrock, the rise of the middle class and the deemphasis of military endeavor as the touchstone of the noble life, or triumphantly put a period to the heroic tradition, ended it with a fully self-conscious flourish. I am more inclined to see Milton as an angel with a flaming sword, forbidding future generations entry into the paradise of epic poetry, rather than as a belated bard, casting about him for materials acceptable to increasingly chubby and unathletic burghers. *Paradise Lost* died in its own fashion, and it took the heroic tradition with it. We shall never look upon its like again: the rest really is silence.

Notes

INTRODUCTION

1   This and all subsequent references to Shakespeare are from the text of the Riverside Shakespeare, ed. G. Blakemore Evans et al. (Boston: Houghton Mifflin, 1974).

2   Thomas Macaulay, *Critical and Historical Essays*, ed. F.C. Montague, 3 vols. (London: Methuen and Company, 1903), 1:16.

3   January 29, 1837. The entry is quoted in *Selections from Ralph Waldo Emerson*, ed. Stephen E. Whicher (Boston: Houghton Mifflin Company, 1957), p. 58.

4   Ralph Waldo Emerson, from the introduction to *Nature* (Boston: James Munroe and Company, 1836), p. 5.

5   For the distinction between remembering and repeating, see Freud's paper of 1914 "Recollection, Repetition and Working-Through," in *The Standard Edition of the Complete Psychological Works of Sigmund Freud*, trans. James Strachey et al., 24 vols. (London: Hogarth Press and the Institute of Psychoanalysis, 1953–1974), 12:145–56. All subsequent references to the works of Freud are taken from this edition, hereafter cited as S.E.

6   The best modern study of the art is perhaps Frances Yeats's *The Art of Memory* (Chicago: University of Chicago Press, 1966). She not only retells the legend of Simonides but also pursues the art of memory through the medieval period to its odd alliance with Hermeticism and Florentine Platonism in the Renaissance.

7 I adapt the term coined by the Prague School to describe certain formalist strategies. See Jan Mukařovský, "Standard Language and Poetic Language" (1932) in *A Prague School Reader on Esthetics, Literary Structure, and Style*, trans. Paul Garvin (Washington, D.C.: Georgetown University Press, 1964), pp. 17–30.

8 The Latin text of the *Aeneid* is quoted from *Vergili Maronis Opera*, ed. F. A. Hirtzel (1900; reprint ed., Oxford: Oxford University Press, 1966). The English translation is Robert Fitzgerald's, *The Aeneid of Virgil* (New York: Random House, 1983). All subsequent quotations of the *Aeneid* in Latin and English are taken from these editions. The line numbers of the Latin text are given first.

9 For an elegant formulation of the argument, see Laszlo Versenyi, *Man's Measure: A Study of the Greek Image of Man from Homer to Sophocles* (Albany: State University of New York Press, 1974), chap. 1.

10 This is similar to the revisionary ratio Harold Bloom calls *apophrades* or "the return of the dead." See *The Anxiety of Influence* (New York: Oxford University Press, 1973), pp. 15–16 and pp. 99–156.

11 Dante Alighieri, *The Divine Comedy*, trans. with a commentary by Charles S. Singleton, Bollingen Series 80, 3 vols.: *Inferno, Purgatorio, Paradiso* (Princeton: Princeton University Press, 1970, 1973, 1975). All subsequent quotations of the *Commedia* in Italian and English are taken from this edition.

12 See Harold Bloom, *A Map of Misreading* (New York: Oxford University Press, 1975), pp. 125–43.

13 *John Milton: Complete Poems and Major Prose*, ed. Merritt Y. Hughes (New York: Odyssey Press, 1957). All subsequent quotations of Milton's poetry are taken from this edition.

I VERGIL

1 *The Odyssey of Homer*, trans. Richmond Lattimore (New York: Harper and Row, 1965). All subsequent quotations from the *Odyssey* are taken from this translation.

2 It seems to me, for instance, that Eric Havelock in his *Preface*

to Plato (Cambridge: Harvard University Press, 1963) takes an extreme position on this matter at the expense of the poems as literature.

3   *The Adventures of Don Quixote*, trans. J.M. Cohen (Baltimore: Penguin Books, 1950), 1.20.

4   It is true that Aeneas's opening sentence recalls Odysseus to Alcinous: "But now your wish was inclined to ask me about my mournful / sufferings, so that I must mourn and grieve even more" (9.12–13). But with the man of many ways, there is always room to suspect the creation of effect.

5   C. P. Segal, "Art and the Hero: Participation, Detachment, and Narrative Point of View in *Aeneid* I," *Arethusa* 14, no. 1 (Spring 1981): 68.

6   Adam Parry, "The Two Voices of Vergil's *Aeneid*," *Arion* 2, no. 4 (Winter 1963): 66–80.

7   For a provocative discussion of narration as repetition and as an attempt at implication, contamination, and seduction, see Peter Brooks, *Reading For the Plot: Design and Intention in Narrative* (New York: Alfred A. Knopf, 1984).

8   S.E. 18:12–17.

9   Steele Commager recently called attention to the complex of terms deriving from *fari* in "Fateful Words: Some Conversations in *Aeneid* 4," *Arethusa* 14, no. 1 (Spring 1981): 101–14. The article stresses the antithesis of *fatum* and *nefas*, an unspeakable sin or abomination, and the ironies implicit in Dido's references to speech. It does not, however, discuss Rumor.

10   In the article cited in the previous note, Commager calls such terms "ancipital words," two-headed words, words that cut in two directions. I focus more narrowly on antitheticals, following Freud in "The Antithetical Meaning of Primal Words" (1910), S.E. 11: 155–61. The essay is a review of a pamphlet of the same title published by the Egyptologist Karl Abel in 1884.

11   E.g., 1. 407–9 (557–61); 2. 790–95 (1026–32); 4. 388–91 (539–42); 6. 467–71 (628–33).

12   That Aeneas's account of his flight from Troy in Book 2 and the

account of his experience in the underworld in 6 share important motifs is argued by Michael C. J. Putnam, *The Poetry of the Aeneid: Four Studies in Imaginative Unity and Design* (Cambridge: Harvard University Press, 1965), chap. 1. The argument suggests that the notion that Book 6 is a "rewriting" of Aeneas's narrative is something more than a metaphor.

13 It has been debated since Alexandrian times whether Homer's episode is really a descent, a true *katabasis* as opposed to a *nekyomanteia*, a conjuring of shades at an oracular site for prophetic purposes. For a discussion of the problem, see Raymond J. Clark, *Catabasis: Vergil and the Wisdom-Tradition* (Amsterdam: B.R. Grüner, 1979), pp. 74–78. Clark's book also contains a discussion of the immensely varied sources Vergil either did draw on or might have drawn on in shaping his sixth book.

14 R. S. Conway, *New Studies of a Great Inheritance* (London: John Murray, 1921), p. 129.

15 *P. Vergili Maronis Aeneidos Liber Sextus*, with a commentary by R. G. Austin (Oxford: Oxford University Press, 1977), p. 218.

16 The problem is chiefly with what the adverb *saltem* modifies. The obvious candidate is *placidis*. T. E. Page insisted that *saltem* must be construed with, and only with, *placidis* and must not be taken with *in morte*. But this yields the constricted and rather weak sense, "That in a home at least peaceful I may rest in death." *Saltem* may modify *quiescam* but probably does not modify the prepositional phrase *in morte*, even though it is here used adverbially. See *The Aeneid of Vergil, Books I–VI*, ed. with an introduction and notes by T. E. Page (1894; reprinted ed., London: Macmillan, 1967), p.469. Austin, *Aeneidos Liber Sextus*, p. 142, says less prescriptively that *saltem* is "probably with *placidis*; after his restless flutterings on the bank of Styx, unburied, it is final peace for which he longs, a peace that so far death has not brought."

17 This is a point made repeatedly and well by Kenneth Quinn, *Virgil's Aeneid : A Critical Description* (London: Routledge and Kegan Paul, 1968).

18 For a lucid discussion of the various abstractions committed on the text of the *Aeneid* in the name of various ideologies, see W. R.

Johnson, *Darkness Visible: A Study of Vergil's Aeneid* (Berkeley: University of California Press, 1976), particularly the first chapter, "Eliot's Myth and Vergil's Fictions."

19 Vergil's revision of the heroic code he found in the Homeric poems has become a critical commonplace, though it is not therefore valueless or untrue. Two books from relatively recent commentators that adopt the argument stand out in my opinion, and the present analysis is indebted to both. They are Viktor Pöschl's *Die Dichtkunst Virgils* (Innsbruck-Wien, 1950), the better part of which has been translated by Gerda Seligson under the title *The Art of Vergil: Image and Symbol in the Aeneid* (Ann Arbor: University of Michigan Press, 1962); and Brooks Otis's *Vergil: A Study in Civilized Poetry* (Oxford: Oxford University Press, 1963).

20 We will return to this question in the concluding section of this chapter.

21 Much labor (and much of it very useful) has been expended on ferreting out Vergil's allusions. G. N. Knauer's *Die Aeneis und Homer* (Göttingen, 1964) is perhaps the most comprehensive gathering. It is well over five hundred pages long.

22 See Austin, *Aeneidos Liber Sextus*, p. 125.

23 I offer my own translation here, because Fitzgerald's translation of *ardens . . . virtus*—"Fiery heroism" (192)—scarcely serves the distinction I argue Vergil is making. Indeed, it begs the crucial question of what we mean by heroism in the first place, one that I argue was very much in Vergil's mind in Book 6 and elsewhere.

24 For evidence that an account of a catabasis of Hercules lies behind this curious inconsistency, see Clark, *Catabasis*, pp. 214–15. Clark argues throughout that the figure of the Eleusinianized Hercules is an important influence on Vergil's conception of his hero.

25 I am indebted to my colleague Thalia Pandiri for drawing this emphatic use of *aeternum* to my attention.

26 It is altogether characteristic of Vergil that he mentions this drugged sop only here and says almost nothing about it. Homer in his circumstantial way would doubtless have told us a good deal more. For

an illuminating discussion of this kind of Vergilian vagueness, see Johnson, *Darkness Visible*, pp. 32–45.

27   The literatue concerned with this mysterious artifact is vast, and the present study is not particularly concerned to survey it or to enter the fray. The great commentary of Eduard Norden, *P. Vergilius Maro Aeneis Buch VI* (1903), 2nd ed. (Leipzig and Berlin: B.G. Teubner, 1916), devotes a long section (pp. 163–75) to the bough and its relation to the folklore of mistletoe, to which plant the bough is compared in 6.205–9. More recent commentary of a more specifically literary kind has produced two essays which I find especially valuable, Robert A. Brooks's "Discolor Aura: Reflections on the Golden Bough," *American Journal of Philology* 74, no.3 (1953): 260–80, and the first part of C. P. Segal's two part article, "*Aeternum per saecula nomen*, The Golden Bough and the Tragedy of History," *Arion* 4, no.4 (Winter 1965): 617–57.

28   For a very suggestive modern interpretation and one that fits my view of the passage and the poem as a whole, see Wendell Clausen, "An Interpretation of the *Aeneid*," *Harvard Studies in Classical Philology* 68 (1964): 139–48.

29   Otis, *Vergil: A Study in Civilized Poetry*, p. 223.

30   The line is in fact a reminiscence of Pyrrhus to Priam in the second book: " 'referes ergo haec et nuntius ibis / Pelidae genitori. illi mea tristia facta / degeneremque Neoptolemum narrare memento' " (547–49).

31   Steele Commager has identified *condere* as an "ancipital," and remarks Vergil's use of it here in *Aeneid* 12. See "Fateful Words," p. 113.

II DANTE

1   C. S. Singleton, *Dante Studies I, Commedia: Elements of Structure* (Cambridge: Harvard University Press, 1954), p.62. In "The Irreducible Dove," *Comparative Literature* 9,1 (1957): 129–35, Singleton succinctly summarizes his influential views of Dante's poetics.

2   Francis Fergusson, *The Idea of a Theater* (Princeton: Princeton University Press, 1949), p. 146. Fergusson has also written persuasively

on Dante's Aristotelianism in *Dante's Drama of the Mind* (Princeton: Princeton University Press, 1953).

3 Leo Spitzer observed: "the whole paradox of *The Divine Comedy* rests in the procedure of describing as real and of conceiving as describable with the same precision as might be applied to an object of the outer world, that which, to our imagination today, would seem to be the product of a gratuitous play of phantasy." See "Speech and Language in *Inferno* XIII," *Italica* 19, no. 3 (September 1942): 87.

4 This and all subsequent quotations from the Bible, except those where the language of the Vulgate is pertinent, are taken from the Revised Standard Version of 1952.

5 I am particularly indebted to John Freccero of Stanford University for first impressing me with Dante's deeply historical imagination. One would have to cite the whole body of Freccero's altogether interesting work on the *Commedia* to show how thoroughly a concern for history pervades his insights. Fortunately, a number of Freccero's pivotal essays have now been conveniently collected in one volume. See *Dante: The Poetics of Conversion,* ed. with an introduction by Rachel Jacoff (Cambridge: Harvard University Press, 1986).

6 Francis Fergusson has prepared an excellent survey and overview of Dante's life and poetry in the first part of his *Dante* (New York: Macmillan, 1966).

7 That Vergil himself was aware of this problem in the poetic character is powerfully suggested by the last lines of his fourth *Georgic*. I am inclined to see him meditating the problem in his retelling of the story of Orpheus (*Georgics* 4.315–527), as well.

8 Freud's theory of sublimation is lucidly set forth in "Psycho-Analytic Notes on an Autobiographical Account of a Case of Paranoia" ("The Case of Schreber" [1911]), S.E. 12: 61ff.

9 These are, of course, the words of Juno. It is further interesting that Freud, a Jew living in an intensely anti-Semitic Vienna, should have chosen as an epigraph for the work that would make his name the words of the champion of the *Semitic* people in the poem. In connection with this, see the anecdote in *The Psychopathology of Everyday Life* (1901) where the young man, in protesting European anti-Semi-

tism, quotes, or attempts to quote, Dido's curse of Aeneas (4.625), s.e. 6: 9.

10   Hjalmar Frisk remarks that the meaning of Erinys is not persuasively explained and lists what I have given here as the first of a number of possibilities. See his *Griechisches Etymologisches Wörterbuch* (Heidelberg, 1960) under "Erinys."

11   The best source of information on the medieval Vergil remains, I think, Domenico Comparetti's *Vergil in the Middle Ages* (1895), trans. E. F. M. Benecke (Hamden, Conn.: Archon Books, 1966). I have gleaned the aspects of the popular account mentioned here from the second half of Comparetti's work, "The Vergil of Popular Legend," pp. 239–376.

12   Ibid., pp. 100–101.

13   T. S. Eliot, "Dante," in *Selected Essays, 1917–1932* (New York: Harcourt Brace and Company, 1932), p. 205. Two critiques of Eliot's position that I have found enlightening are Irma Brandeis's in *The Ladder of Vision* (London: Chatto and Windus, 1960), pp. 130ff., and Glauco Cambon's in *Dante's Craft* (Minneapolis: University of Minnesota Press, 1969), pp. 34–35. The latter is particulary valuable to anyone interested in language in and the language of the *Commedia*.

14   For an extended account of the ways Aeneas may be thought of as a "figure" of Dante the pilgrim, see Robert Hollander's *Allegory in Dante's Commedia* (Princeton: Princeton University Press, 1969).

15   The intensity of Francesca's identification is hinted at by the poet in 5.71 when he speaks of "le donne antiche e' cavalieri" ("the ladies and the knights of old"). It is clear from what the poet tells us later at line 85 that the soul of Francesca is in this group. But the whole rather sordid history of the affair of Paolo and Francesca and their subsequent deaths at the hands of Gianciotto Malatesta, Francesca's husband and Paolo's older brother, was a matter of rather recent memory (the murders took place around 1285), an almost contemporary scandal. Ladies and knights of old had nothing to do with it.

16   For a different account of language as action in *Inferno* 5, see the third chapter of Cambon's *Dante's Craft*, pp. 46–66. Guinevere's smile has been a central subject. Renato Poggioli saw the shift in

terminology from *riso* in line 133, the smile of Guinevere in the romance, to *bocca* in line 136, the mouth of Francesca in life, as "the shift or descent from literature to life, from fiction to reality, from romanticism to realism; or more simply, from sentimental fancy to moral truth." See "Tragedy or Romance? a Reading of the Paolo and Francesca Episode in Dante's *Inferno*," *PMLA* 72, no. 3 (June 1957): 313–58. I would stress the fact that Dante has Francesca's speech come to rest on an image of her mouth, that is, on the source of the speech in the first place. The reminder of the source of speech seriously compromises Francesca's attempt to promote her experience and its retelling to the status of the natural or inevitable.

17   I am indebted once again to John Freccero, who first pointed out to me these correspondences. Note that Dante with his usual precision has even made the numbers of the related cantos correspond: the first allusion to the Vergilian scene occurs in *Inferno* 15, the second in *Paradiso* 15.

18   See Charles S. Singleton in his *Commentary on Inferno* (Princeton: Princeton University Press, 1970), p. 24. For an extended account of the metaphor of the book of memory in Dante's poetry, see Singleton, *An Essay on the Vita Nuova* (Cambridge: Harvard University Press, 1949), pp. 25–54.

19   I have appropriated an impressive phrase from Fredric Jameson here, who foresees the possibility of opening "text and analytic process alike to all the winds of history." See *The Prison-House of Language* (Princeton: Princeton University Press, 1972), p. 216.

20   In "Infernal Irony: The Gates of Hell," *Modern Language Notes* 99, no. 4 (September 1984): 769–86, John Freccero calls attention to Vergil's phrase for the inscription over Hellgate, *scritta morta* (*Inf.* 8.127), "dead writing," language without reference. The essay has been reprinted in *Dante: The Poetics of Conversion*, pp. 93–109. It might be worth comparing the *scritta morta* over Hellgate with the frieze the pilgrim encounters on the Terrace of Pride in Purgatory, which the poet calls *visibile parlare*, "visible speech" (*Purg.* 10.95).

21   Giuseppe Mazzotta has similarly stressed the importance of theft and thievery in this portion of *Inferno* and has drawn the motif into his

fascinating discussion of rhetoric, the dialectic of hiding and re-vealing, the ambiguity of inside and outside inherent in the tongues of flame in *Inferno* 25 and 26. See his "Poetics of History: *Inferno* XXVI,*" *Diacritics* 5, no. 2 (Summer 1975): 37–44, and especially p. 41. An expanded version of this essay has become the second chapter of Mazzotta's *Dante, Poet of the Desert: History and Allegory in the Divine Comedy* (Princeton: Princeton University Press, 1979).

22   The translation is from the RSV and seems to hew closer to the Hebrew than the Douay Version, which has "the house of Jacob from a barbarous people." As the Vulgate follows the Septuagint, Psalm 114 is there numbered 113.

23   See Charles S. Singleton, "In exitu Israel de Ægypto," *Annual Report of the Dante Society* 68 (1960): 1–24. Singleton has been a pioneer in explicat-ing the figural structure of the *Divine Comedy,* and his *Dante Studies I,* and *Dante Studies II: Journey to Beatrice* (Cambridge: Harvard University Press, 1958) should be consulted by anyone interested in this aspect of Dante's po-etics. I still think Eric Auerbach's "Figura" (1944) a central essay in this area. It may be consulted in *Scenes From the Drama of European Literature: Six Essays,* trans. Ralph Manheim, Catherine Garvin, and Eric Auerbach (New York: Meridian Books, 1959), pp. 11–76.

24   Indeed, Dante uses Psalm 114 in explaining to Can Grande his allegorical method in the epistle prefixed to the *Paradiso.*

25   Cambon makes a similar point in *Dante's Craft,* p. 64.

26   My argument elides a stage in the actual history of the word, for Galeotto seems to have shared Pandarus's fate in that his decapital-ized name quickly became a synonym for a go-between. Dante calls Phlegyas, the boatman on the Styx, a *galeoto* (*Inf.* 8.17), where the single "t" may argue that he has only the sense of "pilot" or "oars-man" in mind. Yet I think the word is infected by its appearance in canto 5 and that Dante at least did not mind the reminiscence, for all the infernal go-betweens must have a taint of evil about them, the sense of transporting souls across infernal boundaries for immoral purposes.

27 I say "seems" because of Dante's double relation to Vergil. If Vergil is master and guide of the pilgrim within the fiction, he is still and always the creation of the poet who controls that fiction.

28 For a consideration of periphrasis as a dominant rhetorical figure in *Paradiso,* see Thomas M. Greene, "Dramas of Selfhood in the *Comedy,*" in *From Time to Eternity,* ed. Thomas C. Bergin (New Haven: Yale University Press, 1967), pp. 103–36.

29 Compare the unquestioned acceptance of the pilgrim as poet by the virtuous heathen of *Inferno* 4.

30 For an extended study of the idea of Rome in Dante's poetry and in the Middle Ages, see Charles Till Davis, *Dante and the Idea of Rome* (Oxford: Oxford University Press, 1957).

31 See Singleton's *Commentary on Inferno,* p. 569.

32 Mazzotta remarks in "Poetics of History" that "Dante's own authority is continuously caught between the elusive claim of speaking with prophetic self-assurance and the awareness that this can be a supreme transgression" (p. 41).

33 The best interpretation of the Dark Wood in relation to the poem as a whole is, I think, John Freccero's "Dante's Prologue Scene," *Dante Studies* 84 (1966): 1–25.

34 See Singleton's *Commentary on Paradiso* (Princeton: Princeton University Press, 1975), p. 445.

35 For an excellent brief account of the Ulysses episode and its bearing on all the *Commedia,* see David Thompson, *Dante's Epic Journeys* (Baltimore: Johns Hopkins University Press, 1974).

36 So Hollander seems to take the speech (*Allegory in Dante's Commedia,* p. 174). But Dante was in all probability thinking of Augustine, *Confessions,* 1.8, and the connections he draws in general between the acquisition of language and the development of desire strictly speaking as distinguished from need.

37 For the book topos in medieval literature, see E. R. Curtius, *European Literature and the Latin Middle Ages* (1948), trans. Willard R. Trask (New York: Pantheon Books, 1953), pp. 2–47.

III MILTON

1   For an argument that Milton's thinking *was* genuinely historical and that *Paradise Lost* finds its place in the historical figural tradition of "horizontal" allegory and not in the Platonizing tradition of "vertical" allegory, see William G. Madsen, *From Shadowy Types to Truth: Studies in Milton's Symbolism* (New Haven: Yale University Press, 1968).

2   *Complete Prose Works of John Milton*, ed. Douglas Bush et al., 8 vols. (New Haven: Yale University Press, 1953–80), 1.827. All subsequent quotations of Milton's prose are taken from this edition, and will be cited in the text as C.P.W.

3   On the eve of the Restoration Milton would allude to the whole passage from Samuel in *The Ready and Easy Way to Establish a Free Commonwealth* (1660), but even at this late date he ignores the implications for the Good Old Cause.

4   For an extended meditation on the Miltonic "or," see Leslie Brisman, *Milton's Poetry of Choice and Its Romantic Heirs* (Ithaca: Cornell University Press, 1973).

5   Northrop Frye, *The Return of Eden* (Toronto: University of Toronto Press, 1965), p. 9.

6   "On the Late Massacre in Piemont," Sonnet 18, *Complete Poems and Major Prose*, p. 167.

7   On the question of the inherent metaphoricity of language, see Jonathan Culler, *The Pursuit of Signs* (Ithaca: Cornell University Press, 1981), chap. 10, "The Turns of Metaphor."

8   For a consideration of the similarities between the voice of the narrator and the voice of various characters, see William G. Riggs, *The Christian Poet in Paradise Lost* (Berkeley: University of California Press, 1972). Riggs's argument suggests that, pace Blake, Milton was aware of the risk of joining the devil's party.

9   A. B. Giamatti remarks in *The Earthly Paradise and the Renaissance Epic* (Princeton: Princeton University Press, 1966), p. 298: "In Satan, a major aspect of Milton's style is revealed."

10   One of the finest discussions of the Miltonic narrator, and the

one to which I am particularly indebted, is Anne Davidson Ferry's *Milton's Epic Voice* (Cambridge: Harvard University Press, 1963).

11 Thomas Greene, *The Descent from Heaven: A Study in Epic Continuity* (New Haven: Yale University Press, 1963), p. 404.

12 Eliot's first essay on Milton was contributed to *Essays and Studies* of the English Association in 1936. It may be consulted in *On Poetry and Poets* (New York: Farrar, Straus and Cudahy, 1957), pp. 156–64. His partial recantation of 1947 may be found in the same volume (pp. 165–83). It will scarcely have escaped the reader that the title of the present chapter alludes to Eliot's essay of 1917 "Tradition and the Individual Talent," the first of the essays reprinted in *Selected Essays, 1917–1932*, pp. 3–11. By referring to traditions in the plural, I am suggesting that for Milton tradition was a far less peaceful and unified phenomenon than allowed by Eliot's set of "existing monuments" forming "an ideal order among themselves" (p. 5). We might call Eliot's conception of tradition the High Church view by way of stressing how unacceptable it would have seemed to the deeply Protestant Milton. Eliot, of course, revered Vergil and Dante and disliked Milton. It may be that Milton's pluralistic view of tradition, a consequence of his radical Protestantism, had something to do with this fact.

13 My argument owes much to the approach of Ferry in *Milton's Epic Voice*, pp. 96–97.

14 For an informed account of Miltonic pastoral in *Paradise Lost*, see John R. Knott, Jr., *Milton's Pastoral Vision: An Approach to Paradise Lost* (Chicago: University of Chicago Press, 1971). Though Knott sees Eden as a version of Arcadia, he does not recognize anything demonic in the genre as it is thematized in the poem.

15 Arnold Stein pioneered this line of argument in *Answerable Style: Essays on Paradise Lost* (Minneapolis: University of Minnesota Press, 1953), pp. 17–37.

16 Ariosto, *Orlando Furioso*, ed. Stewart A. Baker and A. Bartlett Giamatti, trans. William Stewart Rose (New York: Bobbs-Merrill, 1968).

17 Joseph Summers, *The Muse's Method: An Introduction to Paradise Lost* (London: Chatto and Windus, 1962), p. 131.

18   Geoffrey Hartman, "False Themes and Gentle Minds" (1968), reprinted in *Beyond Formalism* (New Haven: Yale University Press, 1970), pp. 283–97. The quoted sentence appears on p. 286 of that volume.

19   Greene, *Descent from Heaven*, p. 365.

20   C. S.Lewis, *A Preface to Paradise Lost* (London: Oxford University Press, 1942), p. 97.

21   *Complete Poems and Major Prose*, pp. 63–64.

22   On Milton's enabling "myth" of Shakespeare, see Brisman, *Milton's Poetry of Choice*, pp. x–xi.

23   For some suggestions see John Carey's headnote to Milton's poem in *The Poems of John Milton*, ed. John Carey and Alistair Fowler (London: Longman Group Limited, 1968), pp. 122–23.

24   The translation of Michael Joyce in *The Collected Dialogues of Plato*, ed. Edith Hamilton and Huntington Cairns (New York: Random House, 1961), p. 550. For an excellent discussion of rhetoric in the *Symposium*, and one from which the present argument has benefited, see Helen H.Bacon, "Socrates Crowned," *Virginia Quarterly Review* 35, no. 3 (Summer 1959): 415–30.

25   For a semanticist's view of the present tense in English, see Geoffrey N. Leech, *Meaning and the English Verb* (London: Longman Group Limited, 1971), pp. 1–13.

26   Perhaps the best account of Vergil's manipulation of verb tenses is to be found in Quinn, *Virgil's Aeneid: A Critical Description*, esp. chap. 3.

27   *The Iliad of Homer* (1951), trans. Richmond Lattimore (Chicago: University of Chicago Press, 1961).

28   In *Inescapable Romance: Studies in the Poetics of a Mode* (Princeton: Princeton University Press, 1979), Patricia Parker discusses Milton's moments of suspension and even-ing, like Eve's "staying" before her image in the pool. For Parker such moments "stand as signs for the interval just prior to decision" (p. 123), and they can also have an altogether benign mediating quality, interposing a gradual transition in what might otherwise be a violent break. My discussion of suspension has more to do, however, with the moments after, not prior to decision.

29   *Complete Poems and Major Prose,* p.209.

30   R. W. Smith, "The Source of Milton's Pandaemonium," *Modern Philology* 29, no. 2 (November 1931): 187–98.

31   *Complete Poems and Major Prose,* pp. 68–76. I am aware that in "Il Penseroso" the pensive man imagines himself "in some high lonely Tow'r," but again the poem comes to rest in the "Mossy Cell." For a discussion of towers in the pair of poems, see Cleanth Brooks, "The Light Symbolism in 'L'Allegro-Il Penseroso,' " *The Well Wrought Urn: Studies in the Structure of Poetry* (New York: Harcourt, Brace, and World, 1947), pp. 50–66.

32   Northrop Frye, *The Great Code: The Bible and Literature* (New York: Harcourt Brace Jovanovich, 1982), p. 83.

33   A similar point is made by Stanley Fish, *Surprised By Sin* (1967; reprint ed., Berkeley: University of California Press, 1971), pp. 313–14.

34   For a fuller description of this process, see Louis L. Martz, *Poet of Exile: A Study of Milton's Poetry* (New Haven: Yale University Press, 1980), pp. 189–92.

35   S.E. 18: 36, 38.

36   Ibid., p. 39.

37   Harold Bloom, *A Map of Misreading* (New York: Oxford University Press, 1975), pp. 125–43.

38   Lewis, *Preface to Paradise Lost,* p. 125.

39   Greene, *Descent from Heaven,* p.409.

40   See Alistair Fowler's note to 12.644, in *The Poems of John Milton,* p. 1060.

41   On Milton's insistence that his poem tells the universal story of the sufferings of us all, as opposed to merely the *algea* of Odysseus or the *casus* of Aeneas, see Davis P. Harding, *The Club of Hercules: Studies in the Classical Background of Paradise Lost* (Urbana: University of Illinois Press, 1962), pp. 34–35.

CONCLUSION

1   Peter Brooks, "Freud's Masterplot," *Yale French Studies* 55/56 (1977): 280–300. A version of this essay appears in Brook's recent and extended study of plotting, *Reading For the Plot.*

2   Brooks, "Freud's Masterplot," p. 292.

3   Ibid., p.299.

4   *Homeri Opera* (1902), ed. David B. Munro and Thomas W. Allen (Oxford: Oxford University Press, 1966).

5   See George Dimock's interesting discussion in "The Mistake of Aeneas," *Yale Review* 64, no. 3, n.s. (Spring 1975): 334–56.

6   Walker Percy, "Metaphor as Mistake," *Sewanee Review* 66, no. 1 (1958): 79–99. This essay is reprinted in *The Message in the Bottle* (New York: Farrar, Straus, and Giroux, 1977), pp. 64–82, along with Percy's other interesting and idiosyncratic essays on language and semiotics.

7   Christopher Ricks, following Hume's gloss, makes this point in *Milton's Grand Style* (1963; reprint ed., London: Oxford University Press, 1967), p. 65.

8   Bloom, *A Map of Misreading,* p. 133.

Index

Achilles, 42, 163, 188; as model for Turnus, 52, 53; Priam and, 177–79; shield of, 11–12

Adam and Eve, 146, 164; expelled from Paradise, 165–66, 168–69, 180–81, 182

Adam in *Paradise Lost*, 124, 125, 127–28, 133, 138; fallen speech of, 129, 130–31, 135, 176. *See also* Eve in *Paradise Lost*; Naming

Adamo of Brescia, 13, 101

Ad Herrenium (anonymous), 10

Aeneas, 4, 179; descent of, to underworld, 30, 31–32, 112, 187–88; encounter with Charon, 44–47; expelled from Troy, 181–82; as hero, 38–39, 46, 47–48; historical destiny of, 62, 63, 79; longing for Anchises, 33–34, 36; repetition and, 184, 185; as storyteller, 23–26; suffering of, 41–42, 73, 74, 149, 150. *See also* Dido; individual authors and works

Aeneid (Vergil), 4, 5, 12, 73, 97, 106, 181; allusions to Greek tragedy in, 184–85; as encomium of Augustus, 53–54, 56; founding and naming in, 107–8; Homeric influence in, 39–42, 186, 187; open-endedness of, 58–59; past and future in, 31–33, 38; storytelling in, 17–18; symmetries in, 52–53; world of, 29

Aeschylus, 64, 65

Alcinous, 20

Allecto (fury), 58

Allusions, 170, 177, 184. *See also* individual authors and works; Naming

Amphiaraus, 109

Anachronisms, 4–5

Anchises, 12, 26, 50–51, 53, 81. *See also* Aeneas

Ancients and moderns, 12, 13

Ancient Wood, 63

Andromache, 54

Angels, 94, 95. *See also* Fallen angels

Animism, 131, 132

215